FALLEN SHEPHERDS

Scattered Sheep

A Time for Spiritual Renewal

F. LaGard Smith

HARVEST HOUSE PUBLISHERS
Eugene, Oregon 97402

FALLEN SHEPHERDS, SCATTERED SHEEP

Copyright © 1988 by Harvest House Publishers
Eugene, Oregon 97402

Library of Congress Cataloging-in-Publication Data

Smith, F. LaGard (Frank LaGard), 1944-
  Fallen shepherds, scattered sheep: a time for spiritual renewal
     p.   cm.
   ISBN 0-89081-701-4
   1. Clergy—Conduct of life. 2. Clergy—Religious life. 3. Christian
life—1960-   I. Title.
  BV4325.S55   1988
  253'.2—dc19   88-17644
                       CIP

Dedicated to my brothers-in-law,
Elden, Wilbur, Paddy, and Keith,
who know the challenges and rewards
of spiritual leadership.

With appreciation to
Shirley Roper, David Davenport,
Bill Henegar, and Gary Collier.

Contents

1. Big Scandals, Little Scandals 9

2. A Night of Anguish 15

3. How the Mighty Are Fallen! 29

4. Silent Falls 47

5. Hidden Falls 65

6. The Trouble with Second-Best 79

7. The Superstar Syndrome 93

8. Problems in the Parachurch 111

9. From Soulmates to Bedmates 127

10. Good Man of God, Bad Man of God 145

11. Forgiving, Forgetting, Forbearing 165

12. Who Is Equal to Such a Task? 181

13. Fallen Ministries, Renewed People 197

My people have been lost sheep;
    their shepherds have led them astray
    and caused them to roam on the
        mountains.
They wandered over mountain and hill
    and forgot their own resting place.
Whoever found them devoured them;
    their enemies said, "We are not guilty,
for they sinned against the Lord, their true
        pasture,
    the Lord, the hope of their fathers."

—Jeremiah 50:6,7

1

Big Scandals, Little Scandals

Televangelists, Local Preachers, You and I

If only it were just big-name televangelists. But it was also the respected president of a vibrant Christian fellowship who fell into an illicit relationship and then out of his ministry. And a Christian college president who stepped down when his administration was tainted by his wife's infidelity. And the Catholic priest in Los Angeles who sexually molested a dozen innocent altar boys. And the bestselling Christian author who left his wife for another woman.

The list seems endless. There's the local preacher who turned out to be an alcoholic. The elder who beat his wife and molested his children. The deacon who embezzled church funds. The single Sunday school teacher who became pregnant. The youth minister who shattered the idealism of hundreds of admiring kids when, faced with moral embarrassment, he committed suicide.

You've read about them, heard about them, known them, lived with them—perhaps *been* one of them. They are among the many spiritual leaders over the years who have fallen into disgrace. They've shocked us, angered us, disappointed us. We've felt let down. Cheated. Betrayed.

It's not that apostasy, moral failure, or even maniacal behavior in the name of God is anything new, of course. Which of us can forget the scenes of mass suicide which were broadcast into our living rooms from Guyana? Clearly Jim Jones was a worst-case scenario of a spiritual leader gone bad. But it has never been necessary to go that far.

From *The Scarlet Letter* to *The Thornbirds*, writers have memorialized in fiction what Elmer Gantry's legendary womanizing supplied in real life: a popular story-line in which men and women of God engage in forbidden relationships. Of course, the scandal is not always sexual. There's the former Christian talk-show host and minister of a large Southern California congregation who recently absconded with hundreds of thousands of dollars from church funds. And, although not tainted with similar criminality, Oral Roberts has embarrassed many evangelicals, and even some of his own people, with his "God's-going-to-call-me-home" appeal.

Fallen Biblical Heroes

Lest we lose all perspective, there's the case of Judas to consider. Talk about scandal! Judas was one of the chosen twelve. As it turned out, he was an embezzler and the best-known traitor in all of history, but are we to presume that the remaining 11 apostles were not shocked to learn of his true character? Had he not labored with them side by side in the Lord's work? Had he not participated in their teaching, praying, and baptizing? Had not the crowds following Jesus regarded Judas as a spiritual leader of high rank?

There's also that aching one-liner from Paul to Timothy about the spiritual fall of Paul's co-worker, Demas. He has deserted me, bemoaned Paul, "because he loved this world." How many spiritual leaders have deserted us—and the Lord—because the power, prestige, and pride of this world have crowded out their commitment?

At this point we turn to a different category altogether, but how can we ever forget Peter's darkest day? He who would later proclaim Jesus' lordship with courage and boldness, he who was to become one of the pillars of the church, he who stands out in our minds as one of the greatest spiritual leaders of all time—this same Peter weakened under the pressure of the occasion and denied even knowing Jesus. And he did it not once and softly, but again and again, with loud oaths and curses such as might be expected of a swarthy fisherman, not of a companion of the Savior and a preacher of the Holy Word.

Nor was Peter alone in his attempt to put as much distance as possible between himself and Jesus. For in the garden where Jesus was arrested, *all* the disciples fled! Are we more shocked at the moral failure of spiritual leaders today than we would have been in the first century to read headlines in the Jerusalem *Daily News:* "Popular Religious Leader Arrested, Key Staff Members Disown Him"? If our answer is yes, is it because there is a difference between specific moral failure on one hand and crises in courage on the other? Is it because we can see in retrospect how fallen spiritual leaders, emboldened by the Holy Spirit, found uncommon courage in proclamation of the good news?

Even if we see distinctions between the apostles and modern-day spiritual leaders who have fallen, can we easily explain the sins of those who are honored among the heroes of faith? What of the drunkenness of Noah, or the deception by Abraham, Isaac, and Jacob? Perhaps no spiritual leader could claim as loyal a devotion to God as Moses, yet he too fell victim to the sin of disobedience, thereby subjecting himself to God's discipline.

And as much as we like to believe that the judges during the conquest of Canaan were outstanding spiritual leaders, the plain truth is that many of them would have been a great embarrassment to us today. We hardly need go further than Samson—a man who figured prominently in Israel's history but who brought little in godly character to his role.

Of course, the prime example of a fallen spiritual leader is King David. Guilty of adultery, deception, and murder, David makes even the prominent scandals of our time seem tame by comparison. The Kansas preacher who recently killed his wife in order to marry the church secretary is as close as we've come in a long time. Yet somehow we are able to take David's shocking conduct in stride, as if it were the stuff of which great heroes are made. Somehow David's character is actually enhanced by his great sin and subsequent contrition!

Current Scandals and Scars

So why the difference? Why do we feel comfortable with Moses, David, and Peter—not to mention Solomon, or a host of Israel's kings who sometimes lapsed into idolatry—yet shriek in horror at the scandals which have dominated the press today? Is it because we are identified more closely with the spiritual leaders of our day and along with them are tarnished in the eyes of a world eager to condemn all Christians? Has their black eye become our black eye? Has their dirty laundry ended up in our basket?

Or is there in fact a greater perniciousness about the recent televangelist disclosures? Is there today a sense of hypocrisy or political intrigue which was missing in the lives of those who grace the biblical hall of fame? Indeed, with the global impact of televangelism, are the stakes higher now? Is the Christian community under greater scrutiny because of Watergate, Irangate, and the disaster of Gary Hart? Have we become special targets of a secular society which *wants* us to self-destruct?

Even if we could come to some conclusion—favorable or unfavorable—about those caught up in major scandals, how are we to respond to fallen spiritual leaders within our own churches? There's still the local minister to consider. Do we restore him with extraordinary forgiveness or single him out for special discipline? How do we treat the elder who, instead of leading us, has himself strayed from the path? Must these step down from their positions of leadership, and if so, for how long?

And who, after all, is in fact a spiritual leader? Is it just well-known televangelists and those who would be considered "clergy"? Is it only those who occupy recognized positions within the church? Could it not be said that in one way or another *all of us* are leading others spiritually? Are we not leading our neighbors by the lives we display before them each day? Are we not seen as spiritual leaders in our workplaces and even in our homes?

If we ourselves are also spiritual leaders, in what ways do *we* fall? In what ways do *we* bring disgrace on the church? How have *we* dishonored the name of Christ among those who look to us as spiritual examples? Indeed, what should be done with *us* when *we* fall?

The Crucial Questions

As tough as all these decisions are, there are even more important questions to be asked. Forget the big-name scandals; forget the press-pleasing publicity. Why does disgrace come so easily to the Christian community? Can we stop it from happening again? The answers are not likely to be found by second-guessing individual cases. A closer look at the bigger picture may be far more productive.

Are recognized spiritual leaders even more vulnerable than the ordinary believer? If so, what special temptations do they face? Does the person in the pew contribute to the downfall of those who lead them? Is the church in any way responsible for the disgrace which has been heaped upon it by the actions of a few?

In this book we will explore all these questions in an effort to get a better handle on why spiritual leaders fall and what our response ought to be when they do. More important, we will attempt to discover if there are ways in which we might prevent such falls from ever occurring. In the wake of scandal, we can ill afford to ignore the issues.

What follows at the end of this and each succeeding chapter are questions designed to challenge us in our own personal growth and maturity as Christians. For when all is said and done, it is not the spiritual fall of a leader whose face we have seen only on television that really matters, but the face we see in the mirror each morning. Are you and I growing as Christians? Is our daily walk with God what it ought to be? Is it all that it *can* be? Is there anything we can learn from the spiritual falls of others to help us in our own lives?

From those in the pulpit to those of us in the pew— when spiritual leaders fall, it is a time for personal renewal.

Looking Within

- In what ways have you been affected by the fall of prominent spiritual leaders?

- How are their falls different, if at all, from the falls of great men and women of faith in the Bible?

- In whose eyes would you be considered a spiritual leader?

- What kind of influence do you think you have as a spiritual leader?

- What is the greatest threat to your ability to influence other people for good?

2

A Night of Anguish

The Value of a Good Reputation

What I did was born out of poor judgment—in fact, sheer stupidity, to be honest—but it had every potential for looking far worse than it actually was if taken out of context and construed in the worst possible light against me. And of course that's exactly what happened.

It wasn't long before the phone rang, and I was confronted by an irate friend demanding to know what in the world I was thinking about when I did it. On the face of it, I was defenseless. If all the facts were known, I was sure everything could be cleared up. But I was so embarrassed about what I *had* done that I could only manage to mumble something about being sorry, without attempting to present what evidence there was in my favor.

"Could I come over and talk to you about it?" I asked anxiously. "No," came the reply. "I just can't deal with it right now," he said. "We'll talk about it tomorrow." As I hung up the phone, my spirit sank. For the first time in my life I had to deal with the possibility that my reputation would be ruined forever. I was a well-respected person in the community, in the church, and in my profession of law.

What if this gets out of hand? I might be ruined! If I could tell him exactly what happened, I would still look awfully foolish, but at least he would know that it wasn't nearly as bad as it might otherwise appear. But if the rumor ever spread, there would be no way I could catch up with it fast enough to explain what really happened. The stakes were high. My reputation was on the line. It

15

was not to be an easy night.

Between thoughts of ruin and disaster, eventually I managed to fall asleep. But the next day seemed to stretch out endlessly. We agreed to meet for dinner and talk it out. In the meantime I was haunted with questions. Would I be able to explain it sufficiently? Would there be any openness and understanding? Had word already gotten out during the day? Were people already talking about me in that "It-doesn't-surprise-me" kind of way that people talk when the really juicy gossip comes around? What will I do if it all blows up in my face? How could I have been so stupid? If only I hadn't . . .

We met at a crowded coffee shop. My first reaction was the fear that I would soon be pouring out my soul just two feet away from total strangers casually eating hot fudge sundaes. But there was no turning back, and I couldn't stand the thought of waiting another minute with my future still in the balance.

When we were seated, there was small talk, and then we gave the waitress our orders. I could feel my stomach tightening and could sense my adrenaline flowing. And then it happened: We talked about it. Just talked about it, reasonably and quietly. Our dinners were served, and we kept talking about it—what I had really done, and the feelings which had swirled around me like a storm.

The most important thing I had to get across was that it wasn't nearly as bad as it might easily have appeared. Embarrassing, but not sinful. Beneath me, but not a lapse in moral conduct. Ripe for a ruined reputation, but short of meriting it.

I realize that if I were you, I would be terribly curious about exactly what I did, and I would wonder what, short of actual sin, could be so potentially devastating. You'll simply have to trust me on this one. It was one of those unique circumstances that gave room for great disaster if wrongly interpreted, despite its actual innocence. The sad irony was that I had done far worse things which I am sure had caused God far greater anguish. More than once throughout my life I have found myself struggling and falling because of sin.

But this situation was different, and on this night, praise God, I was looking into the face of a friend with openness and trust in his heart. There was understanding and acceptance, Christian love and forgiveness of my foolishness. What a sense of relief! Like a hostage set free. Peace of mind, like a gentle wave refreshing you from head to toe.

Out of this experience I discovered a new person within me—more concerned, more committed, more careful. No—more full of care for all of us who do things which are beneath us, and for all of us who sin.

It's been several years now, but I still think back on that day of potential dishonor and wonder what might have been. In the years since then I have written several Christian books, for which I have received hundreds of letters expressing appreciation. Some people are kind enough to say that one or another of my books has changed their life and brought them closer to God. What they mean, of course, is that I have brought them to the Word of God, which itself has brought the power of the Spirit into their lives. But I'm grateful to have been the instrument through which God has touched their lives.

Yet it could all have been quite different. Even without complete justification, for a long night and day I had looked scandal in the eye. I had opened the door of disgrace and taken more than a peek at it.

Suppose there had been a different ending to the story. I'm not so vain as to think God could not have chosen another person to write the books I have written. Sometimes I think God has used that experience, as well as my sins, to help me reach out to those who struggle with sin and the human predicament, as I struggle. Perhaps it is why I feel qualified to write this book. I certainly can identify with the more well-known who have fallen, and with the apostle Paul himself when he wrote with obvious inner anguish:

> Christ Jesus came into the world to save sinners—of whom I am the worst. But for that very reason I was shown mercy so that in me, the worst of sinners, Christ Jesus might display his unlimited patience as an example for those who would believe on him and receive eternal life (1 Timothy 1:15,16).

But God's work could have been done without me, and almost was. It would have taken very little to destroy any potential I may have for strengthening other people's lives.

Fragile Reputations

Spiritual leadership—whether in a local congregation, or through a television ministry, or even through Christian authorship—depends on trust and respect, which can be destroyed instantly and permanently by a bad reputation. In *Insights for Today* I arranged the Proverbs topically and wrote devotionals to accompany each day's reading. Because as a Christian writer I am particularly vulnerable in the area of reputation, I have read Solomon's words over and again:

> A good name is more desirable than great riches; to be esteemed is better than silver or gold (Proverbs 22:1).

In the chapter in which that proverb was included, I wrote with the pen of frightening experience when I said, "God is concerned with our good reputations and how easily and irrevocably we can lose them."

I sometimes think that, but for the love of those with whom I live and work on the campus of Pepperdine University, I would long ago have been drummed out of the corps. It was Jesus who said, "A prophet has no honor in his own country." I've often wondered if that isn't because it is in one's own backyard that people really know you, warts and all.

Who knows best the moral weaknesses of the "godly" elder, but his wife and children? Who knows best the wild oats sown by the popular young evangelist, but those in his own neighborhood where he grew up? Can they possibly appreciate the good influence he is now having on thousands of souls?

But sometimes one's backyard is the whole world. Private lives are almost a thing of the past. Moreover, as many people have discovered, a bad reputation can almost never be overcome. With but few exceptions, it is chiseled into one's gravestone forever. One's spiritual fall may be forgiven, but it is rarely forgotten. Once again Solomon confirms the inevitable:

> . . . do not betray another man's confidence,
> or he who hears it may shame you
> and you will never lose your bad reputation
> (Proverbs 25:9,10).

The most amazing thing is how some spiritual leaders think that disgrace will just vanish into thin air, that if they just put out enough propaganda, we will overlook their sin and get on with business as usual—right now, in a hurry, whenever they want it to happen. But good reputations, which take years to build, invariably take even longer to rebuild.

Recognized spiritual leadership is a transparent fishbowl in which reputation is an occupational hazard. The average Christian in the pew perhaps doesn't fully appreciate the scope of the risk for those standing more directly in the spotlight.

All of us sin, and many among us fall. A ruined reputation is devastating to anyone. But do we all run the risk of losing our jobs if our reputations were destroyed? Would our names appear in print in even the local newspaper, much less nationwide? Or in Christian magazines, or on Christian radio? Would our circle of friends be drastically reduced? Would our status within the church be altered in any way? It is the recognized spiritual leader who feels most keenly the real agony of reputations ruined.

There's something else about the reputations of spiritual leaders. Unlike in baseball, where a reputation for losing made the "Cubbies" all the more lovable, bad reputations for spiritual leaders are dead-end streets. There are no "Wait-until-next-year" hopes for the fallen minister. Unlike in politics, where a disgraced Richard Nixon can at least make his way back onto the speaker's circuit, bad reputations for spiritual leaders seldom allow for regained credibility. And unlike the world of Hollywood celebrities, who often bask unashamedly in the floodlight of wretched reputations, bad reputations for spiritual leaders seldom lead to return performances. Rarely are there any second chances.

It's not so much that Christians are less forgiving than those in a secular society. It's simply that moral persuasion is inextricably tied to personal example. If you are not preaching, most people would say you don't have to practice anything. But if you *are* preaching, then most people expect you to practice what you preach. And this is a reasonable expectation even if not always perfectly attainable by preachers, elders, and Bible class teachers (who are, after all, human). It is reasonable because it is what God expects of spiritual leaders. "To whom much is given, from him much will be required."

Because reputations are so fragile, and the consequences irrevocable, those of us who are in positions of leadership—which, of course, means *all* of us in one sense or another—must renew our efforts to guard ourselves from public shame, to avoid the very appearance of evil—not by way of subterfuge, but by candor and openness, so that we are letters of good example, known and read by all men. Like Timothy, we must "set an example for the believers in speech, in life, in love, in faith and in purity" (1 Timothy 4:12). This is a tall order, to be sure, but one to which we must recommit ourselves over and over again.

The apostle Paul was constantly concerned about pure doctrine. Yet his admonition to Timothy about the importance of a leader's personal example is good advice to us as well: "Watch your *life* and doctrine closely. Persevere in them, because if you do, you will save both yourself and your hearers" (1 Timothy 4:16). For Paul, pure doctrine and pure lives were tied together.

Ruining God's Reputation

In this sense perhaps we have missed the real issue about the importance of reputations. So far we've been talking about how a bad reputation can ruin a spiritual leader. But Paul suggests that our reputations are of even greater importance to *God* and to his work in saving souls.

How many people use our ungodly lives as an excuse for ignoring their own spiritual responsibility! How many souls reject Jesus Christ because of what they see in us, his followers! How many of the spiritually blind will stumble over the bad reports they hear about who we really are! Reputations are important for the saving not only of ourselves but also of those whom we might influence for good.

Although a good reputation is important in order to maintain one's position of influence within the church, there is a sense in which one's reputation among those who are outside the church is even more important. Paul supplies the reason in his writing to Timothy about the qualifications for those who would be spiritual overseers: "He must also have a good reputation with outsiders, so that he will not fall into disgrace and into the devil's trap" (1 Timothy 3:7).

Disgrace—that's the word which the world most loves to hear about those who profess Christianity. It confirms their hope that we are wrong in thinking we can rise above common humanity and become truly righteous. And if *we* can't do it, why should they even try? Our scandals justify their sin. Our disgrace covers up their own. So it won't do at all for the most visible among us in the eyes of the world—our spiritual leaders—to disgrace the cause of Christ through bad reputations. Nor will it do for the rest of us to drag Christ's holy name through the mud of our own sins.

Breathtaking Hypocrisy?

There may be still another angle here. Have you ever considered the possibility that the standards of the world may be higher than the standards we ourselves expect within the Christian community? Not their personal morality, but their call for consistency and honesty—at least *from us*. Even if they are proceeding from self-serving motives, they may be quicker than we are to demand that we practice what we preach.

For example, in *People* magazine's article on "The Fall of Jimmy Swaggart" (March 7, 1988), one sentence in particular reached out for my attention. I read it over and over. It followed *People*'s coverage of Swaggart's much-publicized confession and the warm reception it had received from most of those in the audience that day. The sentence was this: "Outside Swaggart's field of of influence, the hypocrisy of his situation seemed breath-taking." Breathtaking hypocrisy—what a stinging indictment!

Whatever one might feel about Jimmy Swaggart, *People* writer Joanne Kaufman was holding him to a higher standard of consistency between his teaching and his practice than what she observed from those within his own congregation. Certainly we may say that Ms. Kaufman might not have considered the element of Christian forgiveness. (I have no idea what her religious beliefs may be.) And perhaps what she intended was merely a cheap shot. But it is also possible that what she said was an accurate reflection of what most people in the world were thinking, especially those outside the Christian community.

If we are to let our lights so shine that others, seeing our good works, will glorify God, the inevitable result of tarnished reputations within the church is the rejection of our God by those on the outside. And it does not matter that they may have judged us unfairly. Nor does it matter that the world thrives on its own hypocrisy. What matters is that we give them no cause for stumbling, no excuse to reject the message we bring, no reason to miss the Person of Jesus Christ.

Have we indeed allowed ourselves to become spiritually complacent about our own lives and the lives of our spiritual leaders? Have we been too gentle with those who share a common faith? In short, have we allowed our hypocrisy to become breathtaking even to the secular mind? Our reputations to those outside are either a barrier or a bridge. Which way has the traffic been flowing lately?

How We Can Help

While the spiritual leader has the central responsibility for maintaining both his personal righteousness and his reputation for righteousness, those who surround him and who look to him for spiritual strength must assume the responsibility for providing a support base of love and understanding. It's not a one-way street: "Freely you have received; freely give."

I can't tell you how very much I appreciate the letters I receive in which some unknown reader not only thanks me for my books but also tells me I am in his or her prayers. One might dismiss the casual "I'll be praying for you" as so much God-talk. But I believe that those who correspond with me sense that I am on the firing line and in special need of God's strength and guidance. Mutual support is why God puts us in families. Mutual support is why God joins us together in the church.

If you do not consider yourself a spiritual leader in the traditional sense, you nevertheless have an important role to play: Pray for those who lead you. Pray not only for their public success with the Word, but for their private battles which you may know nothing about. They all have them. Sometimes they have even greater battles than most people. Many times they win; sometimes they lose. Regard them as if they had overcome; pray for them as if you knew they were losing.

And when you consider your own example at home, in the workplace, and in the community where you live, give thought to your own private battles with sin. Have you prayed about them lately? If you have overcome many temptations in your life, are there others to which you still succumb? Are there sins in your life which hinder your ministry to those who scrutinize your Christian walk? Sometimes we are the only ones who know our private battles. Sometimes we alone can turn our hearts and lives back to God. So encourage *yourself* as well as those who lead in more visible ways.

Haste May Waste

Reputations are treasures in the hands of others. We never hold them for ourselves. After all, we *know* who we are. We know all there is to know—the good, the bad, and the ugly. For us, it's not secondhand speculation or biased conjecture. Therefore, the reputations of those who lead us spiritually are often less within their own control than within ours. As Paul told Timothy, "The sins of some men are obvious, reaching the place of judgment ahead of them" (1 Timothy 5:24). But what of those situations where only *we* are aware of a leader's sin? Does our awareness always merit the leader's exposure? Or is quiet confrontation, confession, and prayer a better option?

To what extent do we contribute to a spiritual leader's bad reputation? Can we make a difference? Should we even try to make a difference? If a leader has made his own bed, should we insist that he lie in it forever? Or is it possible that, through love, we might be able to cover a multitude of sins? Or have we for lesser reasons merely *covered up* sins which should have been exposed?

I find it interesting that Paul's pastoral instructions to Timothy contain dual responsibilities in contiguous sentences:

> Do not entertain an accusation against an elder unless it is brought by two or three witnesses.

and

> Those who sin are to be rebuked publicly, so that the others may take warning (1 Timothy 5:19,20).

There may be occasions to publicly disclose and publicly rebuke the spiritual leader, and we will consider those issues in a later chapter. But in discussing reputations it is intriguing that Paul would seem to suggest that recognized spiritual leaders deserve an extraordinarily high degree of protection from false accusations. Is that because Paul was sensitive to the many false charges and rumors which had been spread about himself? Is it because spiritual leaders are such easy targets? Or is it because of the inevitability of human failure matched against the ongoing need for human spiritual leaders?

Whatever may be the reasons for Paul's instruction, it is God's will that we proceed with all caution when the reputations of spiritual leaders are entrusted to us. I hope it is not just self-serving when I look back in gratitude on the times when my own ministry could have been derailed by uncaring friends and associates, but when instead I found love, understanding, and patience. I thank God that they did not eagerly take advantage of my weaknesses, but rather salvaged the good within me and drew me higher.

Solomon knew the hard truth about the perpetuation of rumors and the risk of reputations: "The tongue has the power of life and death" (Proverbs 18:21). Spiritual leaders can, and too often do, self-destruct. These days we are all too painfully aware of how easily it can be done. The fallen leaders bear personal responsibility for their own sin, but sometimes it is we ourselves who hold within our hands the fate of those who have great potential for good in the kingdom.

Shall we stand ready to condemn? Shall we make it our goal to expose? Or shall we seek to protect where protection is warranted? Is there a way we can stop ill-founded rumors about those to whom we look for leadership?

Whose reputation is in our hands today?

There are many hard questions for all of us to ask in the wake of scandal. If a spiritual leader has fallen, could we ourselves have prevented it through a loving confrontation? Do we ourselves have any role in protecting the reputation of the church? Surely little has changed since the beginning: We are *still* our brother's keeper, even if he is our leader.

Looking Within

- If you were to let your good reputation slip away, how would your life change?
- What contribution to the cause of Christ would be lost if your reputation were ruined?
- In what ways might you blemish God's reputation?
- How can you protect another person's valuable reputation?
- Which are you more concerned about—the purity of your doctrine or the purity of your life?

3

How the Mighty Are Fallen!

The Danger of Pride

During the flight I was busily typing away on my little lap-top computer, which has become my constant traveling companion. At 30,000 feet I was in my own little world, massaging another manuscript to get just the right word at just the right place. The comma I had decided was absolutely necessary yesterday was tossed out today like an unwelcome intruder.

When it came time to "put your seatbacks and tray tables in an upright and locked position," I obediently shut down my office in the sky and relaxed for a few minutes as we approached touchdown at the Denver airport. The weary businessman in the window seat next to me was curious about my writing, and even more curious about my subject, which happened to be baptism.

When the inevitable question came as to why I was flying into Denver, I must have once again startled him with my response: "I'm here to appear on a television talk-show regarding my book, *Out on a Broken Limb*. It's a response to actress Shirley MacLaine and her New Age philosophy." From his reaction I could tell that "New Age" sounded to him like just another product to sell, perhaps facial cream or salad dressing. And he wasn't ready to sell it—or, for that matter, to buy it!

After the other passengers pushed their way off the plane, we got up and ambled slowly up the ramp. Glancing ahead of us, I spotted a very distinguished, slightly graying gentleman, decked out in a spit-and-polish chauffeur's uniform, complete with driving gloves and fancy braids. He was holding a framed sign on which was printed "Dr. F. LaGard Smith."

Amused and slightly embarrassed, I turned to my traveling salesman friend and said, "It looks like they've sent someone to give me a lift." The look on his face was clearly a "Who-*are*-you?" look. I didn't have time to tell him that TV network affiliates usually roll out the red carpet for even the least-known guests, among whom I safely qualified.

The chauffeur showed me to the baggage claim area and pulled my bags off the belt as they came around. "Pretty scruffy bags for this kind of special treatment," I thought to myself. But we were soon out the door and up to the arrivals area. I waited at the curb, as instructed, while he went for the car. Naturally it was a stretched limo, gray and sleek.

As it pulled up alongside the curb, my first reaction was to reach out and open the door. But an unfamiliar sense of snobbery quickly vetoed the impulse, and I waited for the chauffeur to come around and open the door for me. As the bags were being put into the trunk, I looked out through the darkly tinted glass, spying several people who were craning their necks and obviously asking themselves, "Who is he?"

As we took off for the hotel, I slowly measured the cavernous backseat, with its built-in bar and private television. I put my hand on the leather seats and wondered if the leather was Corinthian. The Chrysler commercials give us the idea that we all deserve *Corinthian* leather. Whatever it was, it was rich, supple, and very nice!

I like to think of myself as a simple kind of guy, but I thought I might be able to get used to such royal service. Sure, I had ridden in limos before, but this was rather exceptional treatment all around. And it felt good—really good.

We made our way through the suburbs of Denver and down the boulevards graced by those wonderful old houses built in Denver's heyday at the turn of the century. Entering the downtown area of modern steel and glass, we turned into the covered driveway of one of Denver's finest hotels. Once again came the royal treatment. As the door was opened for me, I stepped out to the sounds of "Dr. Smith" this and "Dr. Smith" that. Sweeping into the lobby, I again sensed people making quick glances in my direction, wondering who it was that was getting all the attention. Pretty heady stuff.

At the check-in counter, the staff practically fell over themselves trying to wait on me. "The room is paid for, of course," one staffer said apologetically, "but could we imprint your credit card in the event of extra charges?" I handed her my well-worn VISA card and then signed the guest register.

With the formalities completed, I was once again whisked up to my room—actually *suite* of rooms—having a magnificent, 180-degree view of Denver, with the sunset-splashed Rockies as a backdrop. A generous tip to the bellhop (as if I had tons of money to spread largess along my way), and I was standing alone at last—just trying to soak it all in. Luxuriating in luxury.

I must tell you that by this time I was feeling pretty important. And then the phone rang. It was the young woman at the front desk. "I'm terribly sorry to bother you, Dr. Smith," she said nervously and with great respect. "But I'm afraid your credit card has been rejected for being over limit." Whew! My chest sagged and my mind raced. "So much for being important!" Her words really brought me down to earth, not to mention down 14 stories in order to hand over with embarrassment another credit card.

No, I'm not really the country bumpkin this story might suggest. The Lord has been exceedingly generous in providing me with rich experiences all over the world. I promise you that I travel Second Class, but life has been a First Class adventure for me.

I live and work on a beautiful university campus in Malibu, California. I have been fortunate to be able to do much of my writing in the breathtaking Swiss Alps, in a flower-bedecked village in Germany, and in a quaint Cotswold stone cottage in England. Even as I write these words, I can hear the gentle bleating of sheep on the hillside and see local horse enthusiasts in traditional hunt attire as they head their steeds up the village lane.

More important, I have a wonderful family and a host of friends who fill my life with sharing and caring. I am part of a church fellowship which, if we sometimes exasperate each other, has always been a source of strength and encouragement. I can't even begin to count the number of homes I could walk into on a moment's notice and be treated as one of the family.

The point of the story, then, is not that I had a humbling and amusing experience along an unfamiliar high road of worldly success. The point is that even someone who has been around the block a few times and has tasted of what the "good life" has to offer can still experience the heady wine of special attention.

Pride in Stretch Limos?

On the various promotion tours I made for *Out on a Broken Limb*, I rode in several limos and stayed in many nice hotels. More than once the irony hit me that I was riding in the lap of luxury on my way to talk-shows in which I would point out that thousands of people are turning to the spiritualism of the New Age movement in an attempt to escape from materialism—materialism which they have seen even in the church. And indeed some of my courtesy limos were provided by Christian organizations.

I don't mean to make a big issue over Christian ministries and stretch limos. With as many guests as they have coming in and out of town each day, it may be the most practical way of expediting the various needs involved—although I must say that Doug Walker has taken care of me in sufficiently grand style with his modest, ministry-owned Ford van when I have appeared on "The 700 Club."

Whether it be a limo, a Ford van, or a ministry-owned private plane, my concern is that we too often play to the weakness of spiritual leaders. Leadership of any kind is a heady experience. And spiritual leadership is not exempt. Nor has it ever been. Nor does it take modern affluence to tug on the strings of pride and power which are so intoxicating. Through Hosea, God had said of all his people, not just the leaders:

> When I fed them, they were satisfied;
> when they were satisfied, they became proud;
> then they forgot me (Hosea 13:6).

Like the rest of us, spiritual leaders can become too materially satisfied. Beyond that, the pride which comes before destruction is often the fruit of too much attention, material and otherwise. And it goes almost without saying that the Christians who get most of the attention are our spiritual leaders.

The prophet Isaiah pulled no punches about how low spiritual leaders can fall if being surrounded in luxury goes to their heads:

> Israel's watchmen are blind,
>   they all lack knowledge;
> They are all mute dogs,
>   they cannot bark;
> They lie around and dream,

>   they love to sleep.
> They are dogs with mighty appetites;
>   they never have enough.
> They are shepherds who lack understanding;
>   they all turn to their own way,
>   each seeks his own gain (Isaiah 56:10,11).

Harsh words indeed for lazy preachers, complacent elders, materialistic evangelists, and greedy spiritual leaders of all types! But it is not just the money we might lavish on a few high-salaried televangelists, or even the limos and high-priced hotel rooms that others of us occasionally enjoy. Many fellowships run on shoestring budgets but face the same problem of fallen leaders. The money, cars, and private planes are only symptoms. The real cause for concern is the *attention* which spiritual leaders receive. The praise. The limelight. The reverence. Even the awe.

All Sorts of Limos

Before limos and private jets were ever invented, Jesus said of the spiritual leaders of his day:

> Everything they do is done for men to see: They make their phylacteries wide and the tassels on their garments long; they love the place of honor at banquets and the most important seats in the synagogues; they love to be greeted in the marketplaces and to have men call them "Rabbi" (Matthew 23:5-7).

Has Jesus painted the picture of anyone we know? Are you and I part of the picture? We don't have to be millionaire televangelists to find ourselves reeling from his deft blow. Who among us doesn't like the spotlight?

Who among us doesn't enjoy recognition? How many of us regularly turn down any honors that may come our way? For the vast majority of ministers, who get paid ridiculously low salaries, the honor may be all there is—at least apart from the spiritual rewards.

The truth is that many spiritual leaders fall because they trip on the pride of their ecclesiastical robes and choke on the special recognition which their clerical collars demand. They fall so hard because they have built their pedestals so high.

But there is another side to the robes and rituals story. I discovered it from a passenger on a recent flight who was telling me about the young Methodist minister at her church. It seems he preached a sermon to the effect that he was no longer comfortable with some of the traditional ritual which they observed, including his having to wear a robe while leading the congregation in worship.

"After all," he said, "I am no different from the rest of you. We are all ministers." Not unexpectedly, his sermon didn't sit well with many people in the church. It just didn't seem right to dispense with the robes. It took away from the . . . well, the beauty of the service, they thought.

For every minister and evangelist who loves the pomp and circumstance bolstering his elevated position, there must be many who find it all very oppressive. As one who has participated in an endless number of robed academic processionals, I can tell you that, for all the honor that academic gowns may signify, most of us feel nothing but relief when we finally get to take the stuffy things off! And I can well imagine how much more oppressive clerical robes must be to those who find the symbolism of separateness to be a burden they could do without.

But the surprise is how many people in the pew *want* the robes, *demand* the ritual, and *insist* on the elevation of the clergy because they wouldn't feel comfortable without it. For them it just wouldn't seem like a church if the trappings were taken away. If spiritual leaders love to take the prominent seats, the common folk love to see them there. If spiritual leaders love to be called by special ecclesiastical titles, the person in the pew seems to have a need to call them by those titles. Perhaps there's a kinship with the millions who stay up late to watch royal weddings. How we all love a show!

Have we completely overlooked Jesus' teaching about how we ought to refer to those who lead us?

> But you are not to be called "Rabbi," for you have only one Master and you are all brothers. And do not call anyone on earth "father," for you have one Father, and he is in heaven. Nor are you to be called "teacher," for you have one Teacher, the Christ (Matthew 23:8-10).

Faced with Jesus' own teaching, should we not prayerfully rethink how we address our spiritual leaders? Can we conscientiously keep referring to them as Father MacCready or Reverend Jones? Because Jesus reminds us that we are all brothers, many fellowships have abandoned other clergy-elevating titles, only to lapse into a specialized use of the word "brother." It too has become corrupted, so that we refer to everyone else in the congregation as Pete, and Tom, and Bill, but greet the minister as Brother Jones with a capital "B." Nor can we overlook the titled use of "pastor," a word designating a *role* of leadership, not a special clerical title.

But why all the fuss? What do titles and robes have to do with fallen spiritual leaders? Jesus did not leave us to speculate. On the heels of his admonition about religious titles, he tells us why the seemingly little things are so important:

> The greatest among you will be your servant. For whoever exalts himself will be humbled, and whoever humbles himself will be exalted (Matthew 23:11,12).

When we insist on tagging spiritual leaders with elevated titles, we set them up for a fall. We feed their egos, distort their sense of importance, and rob them of a sense of servant leadership. Other than a spiritual leader, perhaps only an academic can understand how much ego is tied to titles and designations. Even in a Christian university, you would do well to carefully sort out who has a Master's degree and who has a Doctorate. Only at the risk of great effrontery would you address a "Doctor" as a "Mister"!

Of course, my colleagues in the law school where I teach look with disdain on all the academic sensitivity in the undergraduate school about correct titles. As long as our students call us *Professor* Smith and *Professor* Nelson, we couldn't care less!

I well know that warm feeling that comes from being addressed with a term of respect. But why do I accept with ease the "Dr. Smith" which appears on the academic correspondence in my law school mailbox, but cringe when it is used to introduce me as I am about to take the pulpit as a visiting preacher?

In spiritual matters, clerical titles are like verbal limos. Although we may use them with all due respect, we only contribute to the potential for false pride in those whom we admire. After all, who will refuse to go on an ego trip when the ticket has already been paid for? The fact is that spiritual leaders often fall because we give them too much praise and special attention. We do them no favors by this. Our respect can be better shown by honoring the One whom we all serve, Jesus Christ.

Who Is the Greatest?

If our only concern were limos, robes, and clerical titles, the inquiry surely would be too narrow. Those things are simply *part* of the overall problem of pride. Recent publicity has shed light on a bigger part of the problem, which you are likely to find in your own congregation without ever watching Nightline. It's the clamor for power, rank, and position among spiritual leaders.

Just listen to the questions which seem to matter to so many: Who presides over the biggest church or parachurch ministry? Who has the biggest budget and largest donations? Who has brought the most people to Christ in the last year? Whose television or radio program appears in the most markets throughout the country? And, yes, of course—which Christian books have sold the most copies?

Let's bring it even closer to home. Which pulpit minister pleases the most members? Which youth minister is most popular with our young people? Which elder is recognized by the others as being the "head bishop"? Which singer has the best voice? And on it goes. In a competitive society where being at the top is all there is, even the church gets caught up in the pride of asking, "Who is the greatest?"

Pride is an old story, and it has trapped men greater than ourselves, including the apostles who walked the dusty roads of Palestine with our Savior. Had they not heard his Sermon on the Mount in which he said, "Blessed are the meek and the poor in spirit"? When at the transfiguration Peter wanted to erect three shelters to honor Moses, Elijah, and Jesus, had not the voice of God singled out Christ as the only One to be honored? Yet Mark records the infighting among the apostles which took place just days after that glorious event:

> They came to Capernaum. When he was in
> the house, he asked them, "What were you

arguing about on the road?" But they kept quiet because on the way they had argued about who was the greatest.

Sitting down, Jesus called the Twelve and said, "If anyone wants to be first, he must be the very last, and the servant of all" (Mark 9:33-35).

Luke then records the object lesson that Jesus presented to the Twelve so that they might learn the lesson of servant leadership:

> An argument started among the disciples as to which of them would be the greatest. Jesus, knowing their thoughts, took a little child and had him stand beside him. Then he said to them, "Whoever welcomes this little child in my name welcomes me; and whoever welcomes me welcomes the one who sent me. For he who is the least among you all—he is the greatest" (Luke 9:46-48).

Can you believe that even this lesson did not put a stop to the apostles' jockeying for position and power? Some time later James and John approached Jesus and asked presumptuously, "We want you to do for us whatever we ask." I would love to have seen Jesus' reaction to that request! "Let one of us sit at your right and the other at your left in your glory," they went on. But Jesus only reminded them of the baptism of suffering which they would one day share with their Master (Mark 10:35-40).

The postscript to this incident, which I find alternately sad and humorous, would later be recorded with complete candor by Matthew, one of the very ones involved in the disputing: "When the ten heard about this, they became indignant with the two brothers."

Indignant, only because they hadn't thought of the idea first! But once again Jesus patiently explained to them that spiritual leadership is not like the political leadership which they desired:

> You know that the rulers of the Gentiles lord it over them, and their high officials exercise authority over them. Not so with you. Instead, whoever wants to become great among you must be your servant, and whoever wants to be first must be your slave—just as the Son of Man did not come to be served, but to serve, and to give his life as a ransom for many (Matthew 20:25-28).

If only this could have settled the matter once and for all! But it didn't, for even at the "last supper," Jesus' chosen disciples were still arrogantly and pridefully vying for more attention. To be with the Lord wasn't enough. To have been honored as one of 12 men specially chosen as Christ's ambassadors on earth wasn't enough. Incredibly, nothing short of top billing would satisfy them.

Maybe it's the nature of leaders that they must always be at the top. If they weren't good at pushing, maybe the rest of us wouldn't follow. I wish it were just a management principle, free from moral implications. But I'm afraid it is not. And, in the case of his disciples, Jesus was sure that it was not.

If he were with us on earth today, I imagine Jesus telling us that servant leadership makes good sense even in the business world, but is absolutely mandatory in the spiritual realm. If ladder-climbing is helpful in promoting sales, it is disastrous in promoting piety. Our business is conversion, not consumerism.

For us the "last supper" is the occasion of a memorial. For the apostles, it was a spiritual management seminar.

During the meal Jesus got up quietly and began to wash the disciples' feet, performing the task of a lowly household servant. It surprised the apostles, needless to say. They couldn't imagine what in the world had gotten into Jesus: The ultimate spiritual leader, lowering himself to such a humble position!

It must have been even a bit embarrassing even for them—like forgoing the limo for a broken-down bicycle. It didn't make sense. Nor would it, until they had fully learned the lesson of servant leadership. Nor will it for us until we have learned the same lesson.

Naturally, this lesson runs against the grain of our own thinking. When it comes time to appoint elders and deacons, our inclination is to choose men who have been successful in the kind of community of which we are a part. In the urban church, it is the successful businessman. In the rural church, it is the successful farmer. On a Christian college campus such as the one where I teach, it is often the successful university administrator or faculty member.

We tend to associate success in the secular world with probable success in the church, even though that assumption may be far from the truth. The man who climbs the corporate ladder at the office may have great difficulty climbing back down in order to lift others higher.

Why do spiritual leaders fall? Because we've gotten off our knees and tried to stand too tall. We've forgotten our place as leaders. We've forgotten the picture of Jesus, down on the floor with a dirty towel in his hands. That's where he calls us to be leaders.

The path to greatness is downward, not upward. When spiritual leaders fall, it's no wonder we hear someone say, "The scandal has brought him to his knees." When you think about it, the Lord is doing us a favor. On our knees is where we belong in the first place.

Politics in the Church?

What is it that leads us to rally around a particular man of God, as if he were heaven-sent like none other? Why do we seem to need "big-name preachers"? Why is it that we are always on an inevitable slide toward partisanship? We are not considering here those spiritual leaders who go to bed each night counting attendance figures instead of sheep, but the rest of us. As we have seen before, if there are men who seek power and popularity within the church, the rest of us seem to be quite happy to give it to them. If they want a following, we gladly step in line and follow.

But more distressing is the fact that we sometimes form a following for those who don't even *want* one! The Corinthian church provided a classic example. Neither Paul nor Apollos nor Peter was out to see if he could have the most successful ministry. Yet the people in the church were taking sides and pushing for their favorite evangelist. Some said, "Paul is my man"; others said, "Apollos is the best in my opinion"; and others said, "There will never be another like Peter."

It wouldn't take long for most of us to let such adulation go to our heads; it's nice to be appreciated. When my students fill out their faculty evaluation questionnaires, I can forget all the ones which say I should get out of teaching altogether if I can find a few that tell me I'm the best teacher they have.

For spiritual leaders, most of whom get more than their fair share of criticism, it is flattering to have a fan club. And for the rest of us, it is nice to have someone to admire spiritually. I admit that I too have favorites. Some people feed me more than others. Some people, whose righteous lives stand in stark contrast to my own, challenge me to greater spiritual heights than others. If they had fan clubs, I would join. If the fan clubs had officers, I would run for president. They mean that much to me.

Big ministries are usually built by sincere people who fill an important need in our lives. They don't start out with lots of money in the ministry coffers. They don't begin with overflow crowds in Madison Square Garden. They get big because they edify us and we flock to them. It's not their fault that we fill their classrooms and auditoriums to overflowing, or listen faithfully each time they're on the air. But our appreciation can *become* their fault. It can become their temptation to pride. It can turn strength into weakness, sincerity into sin. Ironically, good people can be turned into bad simply by enjoying too much spiritual success.

One of the things I appreciate about the people I work with at Harvest House Publishers is that they really care about what's happening in the Christian community. In a recent conversation, one of the staff expressed a concern that Christian book readers tend to read narrowly from their favorite author. And if their favorite author has said something, it must be true.

I can personally attest to the many letters which I have received which ask for the titles to all the books I've authored. "I want to read everything you've written" is flattering but also scary. And I should think it even more of a problem for authors whose books have sold millions of copies and cultivated cultlike followings. Even a humble man may succumb to the seduction of pride when we constantly push it in his face.

Sometimes leaders fall because we push them too far in the wrong direction. We give them followings they never asked for and wonder why they start to like the idea.

Sometimes we simply push them too soon.

Too Soon the Honor?

When Paul instructed Timothy regarding the appointment of elders, or spiritual overseers, he specifically excluded the novice. "He must not be a recent convert," Paul warned, "or he may become conceited and fall under the same judgment as the devil" (1 Timothy 3:6). The basis for Satan's judgment? Pride. And it is pride that can ruin a good man if he is entrusted with leadership too quickly.

We have seen the same principle at work in inexperienced White House staff members. Seasoned professionals normally can handle the heady powers of state; few green political appointees seem to be able to. All that raw power is intoxicating to the rookies at the helm. We've come to recognize the syndrome as Watergate, Irangate, and heaven-only-knows-what's-next-gate.

You can also recognize victims of the too-far-too-fast syndrome in dustbins at the foot of corporate ladders from which they have fallen, and in the academic obituaries of college administrators who have let early successes literally change who they once were. As tragic as these losses are, nothing can compare with the waste of human potential when a shooting star among spiritual leaders experiences premature burnout.

I've always liked the idea that, for the most part, Jesus chose his apostles from among the common folk. They weren't graduates of the Jerusalem School of Theology, and didn't even have a M.Div. degree. None were well-known theologians, successful evangelists, or highly respected teachers of the law. In fact, Jesus' "short list" included no one from among those whom we would consider today to be among the clergy. Surely he was trying to tell us something with that obvious break from what would have been expected. Yet his decision had a built-in risk factor which, as we have seen, surfaced time and again. Untested men taken to high places are almost certain to slip from the path. And slip they did, over and over.

If spiritual leaders fall, sometimes it is because we give honor to those for whom honor is not yet due.

Leaders Above the Law?

You may have admired Colonel Oliver North. I confess I'm not so sure. But I think even North's admirers would acknowledge that he ran into trouble at the very point where he began to think, for however justifiable a reason, that he was entitled to act above the law. It was almost a flashback to Richard Nixon and "all the president's men." Was that also the point where King David fell? And King Solomon as well?

The problem with pride is that it makes us forget who we are. Through countless little ways we keep telling our spiritual leaders that they are different from us. *They* are clergy; *we* are laymen. *They* are higher; *we* are lower. *They* are special; *we* are ordinary. *They* do the talking; *we* do the listening. *They* wear robes and collars; *we* do not. *They* are called Reverend, Father, Pastor, and Brother; *we* are simply called Christians. Spiritual leaders and spiritual followers are both separate *and* unequal.

It doesn't take long for some spiritual leaders to get the increasingly corrupt message: You are different; you are special; you are an exception to the norm; you play by a different set of rules; you are exempt; you are above the law. As a spiritual leader, you are in a special category. You recognize it, those whom you lead recognize it, and surely God must recognize it.

"After all, I *was* called to the ministry, wasn't I?" And "God knows I'm not perfect, so he must think I'm okay the way I am." And "Maybe he even *allows* me moral lapses in order to relate better to those I'm leading." And "Don't forget how much good I do for the Lord. Surely there's some kind of balance in effect, such that the more good I do, the more moral leeway I am given." And "I *do* need that avenue of escape, because it's not easy being a spiritual leader. Just let all those other folks try being a spiritual leader sometime, and they'll see what I mean." "I'm God's man, and I'm different. I'm God's man, so I can cut corners. I'm God's man, so I'm strong enough to withstand temptations to which others, lesser than myself, would succumb. I'm God's man, so I know what the *real* reason behind the rule is, and therefore the rule doesn't actually apply to me. How do I know I'm God's man? Because everyone keeps telling me I am."

Why do spiritual leaders fall? Because we deceive them about their own humanity. We let them think they walk on water and then act surprised when they drown!

Looking Within

- How do you get into trouble because of pride?
- How does our traditional clergy-laity distinction contribute to the temptations of pride?
- Are there ways to show your appreciation for a spiritual leader without contributing to his own problem with pride?
- Can you think of ways in which you might be a better servant-leader to others?
- How does the affluence of our society affect your ability to serve other people?

4
Silent Falls

Struggles in the Heart

When I was a youngster, our family would pack all six of us into a station wagon, together with a bushel of peas to shell along the way, (Mother took seriously that line about idle hands and the devil!), and away we would go across the great American landscape. Dad used to hold weeklong evangelistic meetings as far away from Texas as Wyoming, Colorado, and California. So our vacations were always made up of the trips going and coming.

Through the years we saw Yellowstone, with Old Faithful, the Mammoth Paint Pots, and lovely Morning Glory Pool; rode the chair lift in the summer up the slopes of the Grand Tetons; ascended Pike's Peak by train; walked nervously across the suspension bridge at the Royal Gorge; and stumbled over the lava rock of a dormant volcano. In New Mexico we chilled our milk in an ice-cold river and visited the ancient cave dwellings of the Pueblo Indians.

But wherever we traveled, I remember being impressed with how many waterfalls we saw—everything from little trickles of mountain water by the side of the road (where we would stop to fill our thermos bottles) to the awesome Yosemite Falls in Yosemite. Of course, there were countless "Upper Falls" and "Lower Falls." It shouldn't have been surprising that they always seemed to come in pairs. The other falls always had such great names: "Inspiration Falls," "Widow Falls," "Horseshoe Falls." And if you've ever driven through the South, you could hardly have escaped one of the many signs inviting you to "See Ruby Falls."

In the years since then I have wondered why we all love falls so much. Is it their aesthetic beauty? Their relative rarity? Or are we drawn to their extraordinary power—power that we can almost touch, particularly in the great falls of the world?

Niagara Falls is probably the best-known of the larger falls. But I have stood at the foot of the mighty Victoria Falls in Zimbabwe, drenched in the spray that hangs like rain in perpetual suspension over the mossy banks where waters from the world's largest waterfall drop with atomic-like force onto the quiet Zambezi River.

I love falls. In nature they are powerful and majestic. But in *human* nature, falls are tragic.

I suspect there may be lessons we can learn from the variety of falls we see about us in nature. There are big falls and little falls. Single falls and series of falls. Famous falls and unknown falls. Advertised falls and falls you discover by accident. Funny falls and scary falls. Natural falls and man-made falls.

It's the same with spiritual falls. They are not all the sensational, Niagara-type falls of a popular televangelist. Nor are they likely to be the scary fall of the murdering minister from Emporia, Kansas. Most of them, in fact, are quiet falls, behind the scenes, known only to a few people. But they all play an interesting part in the interwoven tapestry of our spiritual life together. You may never have the opportunity to see these falls. No one's name will appear in the headlines. But these falls do have names—and faces, and feelings, and families.

They're worth viewing from behind the scenes. Up ahead is the sign: "Come See Silent Falls."

Imagination Falls

The first spiritual falls we come to are found off the beaten track, but you find more of them than you might think. They are falls that are as familiar to the average person in the pew as they are to spiritual leaders. Unfortunately, when found in spiritual leaders, they tend to have a debilitating effect on their ability to lead. If you ever come across them, you probably won't recognize them except for the almost-hidden sign which reads "Imagination Falls."

I recognized one of these falls along my way less than a month ago. I was talking with a friend of many years, going back to when I was a teenager. Now, his own children are teenagers—and out of control. With moist eyes and a breaking voice, he confided, "LaGard, I'm a failure. I've lost touch with my children, and I can't do anything about it." It was a tender moment of confession, and a tearful plea for help. It was an imagined fall of a gentle man of God.

I've always known my friend to be a stalwart brother in the church. He and his lovely wife never miss a service, whether it be a worship service to God or an opportunity to be of service to others. They are faithful, and full of faith. Nevertheless, here he was, haunted by the fear of failure.

We weren't in a position where we could talk long, so I just reminded him quickly of the "good-king-bad-king" phenomenon during the time of the divided kingdom of Israel. Good kings often had bad sons. Bad kings often had good sons. When children go astray, the fault doesn't necessarily lie with the parents.

"Train a child in the way he should go, and when he is old he will not turn from it," is a wise proverb. As with all proverbs, it expresses a worthy ideal and a general truth. But it offers no guarantee of unqualified success— at least not at every stage. Sometimes it takes more maturity, so that the sequel, "when he is *old*," comes into play. Fortunately, many children come back to their senses after scouting out the unfamiliar territory of temptation in younger years.

Yet how many godly parents grieve for their children who have not followed them in the faith, even when graced with maturity! Yet we must all listen carefully, if painfully, to Ezekiel's clear teaching:

> The soul who sins is the one who will die. The son will not share the guilt of the father, nor will the father share the guilt of the son. The righteousness of the righteous man will be credited to him, and the wickedness of the wicked will be charged against him (Ezekiel 18:20).

After parents have diligently and prayerfully taught their children about God, and have lived godly lives in their presence, they have done all that God requires of them. Each person bears his or her own spiritual responsibility before God. And that goes for one's own children as well as for complete strangers.

But I know that's easy to say, especially for someone who is not a parent. And I know there's always that nagging guilt complex, whispering in the back of one's mind, "But maybe you *didn't* teach them diligently and prayerfully enough. Maybe you *didn't* live a sufficiently godly life before them."

If we had the opportunity, we could ask Samuel's mentor, Eli the priest, about those feelings. Surely he had spent many a restless night worrying over his two rebellious sons. Had he not taught them to love God with all their heart? Had he been too busy "doing the Lord's work" to spend time with his sons? Had he been a spiritual leader to everyone but his own children?

I can tell you that Eli is not alone, and neither is my agonizing friend. When preachers' kids go wrong, as they do often enough to give all preachers' kids a bad reputation, there is untold grief in the hearts of those who believe they have succeeded in the pulpit, only to have failed at home.

And the sad truth of the matter is that many parents *have* failed. Preachers, and preachers' wives, have failed; elders and deacons and their wives have failed; Bible class teachers have failed. They have busily taken the Word to others and borne the great burdens of hospitality and concern, but thoughtlessly abandoned their own families. And for them there will come a great day of anguished accounting. But at some point along the way there has to be an end to parental responsibility, even for spiritual leaders.

If most of us think back on how hard our own parents tried to raise *us* up in the nurture and admonition of the Lord, and how many times we've failed *them*, we might begin to understand that parenthood has limited responsibility attached to it.

For spiritual leaders, of course, there is the added burden of appearances. Paul introduces the problem in laying down for Titus the qualifications of spiritual overseers:

> An elder must be blameless . . . whose children believe and are not open to the charge of being wild and disobedient (Titus 1:6).

In writing to Timothy, Paul explained why such importance attaches to a spiritual leader's children:

> He must manage his own family well and see that his children obey him with proper respect. (If anyone does not know how to manage his own family, how can he take care of God's church?) (1 Timothy 3:4,5).

The balance to be struck between one's qualifications for spiritual leadership and his ability to be a good parent may not be as difficult as it first might seem. As we have suggested before, true leadership is not voted in, but earned through respect. Therefore, if a person is held in high respect, despite how one of his children may have turned out, his ability to lead has not been impaired.

This fact won't lessen his personal agony regarding the state of his children, but he should be slow to declare himself a failure, either as a parent or as a spiritual leader. After all, one's call to spiritual leadership ultimately rests in the call of God.

So Many Imagined Falls!

Similar imagined falls also haunt those in roles of responsibility within their local congregations. If the church is stagnant, they feel it's all their fault. If attendance is dwindling, "It must be my preaching," says the weary minister. If problems arise among the members, "It must be my inadequate leadership," says the beleaguered elder. If the children haven't learned their memory verses, "It's my fault," says the worried Sunday school teacher.

Is it any wonder that the ranks of preachers are dwindling? Or that so few godly men are willing to be appointed as spiritual overseers? Or that the turnover is so high among Bible class teachers? Satan hasn't defeated us as much as we have defeated ourselves.

Once again, Ezekiel comes to our rescue. And he knew whereof he wrote. Ezekiel too was a weary, worried, and beleaguered spiritual leader. God spoke both *to* him and *through* him about the responsibilities of leadership:

> Son of man, I have made you a watchman for the house of Israel; so hear the word I speak and give them warning from me. When I say to the wicked, "O wicked man, you will surely

die," and you do not speak out to dissuade him from his ways, that wicked man will die for his sin, and I will hold you accountable for his blood. But if you do warn the wicked man to turn from his ways and he does not do so, he will die for his sin, but you will have saved yourself (Ezekiel 33:7-9).

The role of the spiritual leader is to teach, counsel, and warn. We are not judged for how successful our efforts might be. God has called us to do the planting and the watering, regardless of the increase. When attendance drops and troubles come, certainly we ought to take stock of what's happening and why. But dropping out of a leadership role because nothing seems to work despite our best efforts is giving over to imagined failure. If the apostles—or even Jesus himself—had taken that attitude, Christianity never would have survived.

Self-doubts and unreasonable fears are unnecessary falls. In fact, they are not *falls* at all! If God enlisted only perfect men and women in his service, his work would never get done. The "Imagination Falls" of this life have caused far more destruction than ever warranted. These are "falls" at which we should never stop more than momentarily, and in no case should we allow ourselves the wasteful indulgence of bottling them up inside us.

Secret Falls

The second type of falls which we want to explore are true falls, but also among the most difficult to locate. They are always hidden from public view. Hence the name "Secret Falls." Everyone experiences them, but because they are secret, one can only speculate about how they affect spiritual leadership. What is *not* a secret is that we all have secret sin. Perhaps it is not the dramatic sin of immorality which too often fills the headlines, but it is sin nevertheless—secret sin.

King David's sin with Bathsheba is now legendary. However, until it became public, David's sin was hidden from view. One wonders, of course, how it was ever possible for the king of Israel, surrounded as he must have been by a royal entourage, to pull off the affair without *somebody* knowing. It was as unlikely as keeping a lid on the fact that President Kennedy had a mistress during his term of office—a woman who, as we have learned since, was a personal messenger between Kennedy and certain Mafia figures. In Kennedy's case, scandal was averted by an assassin's bullet. In David's case, the prophet Nathan became God's investigative reporter to blow the whistle.

Surely a member of David's family must have suspected that something was amiss. Surely some security officer must have known of David's whereabouts when David was with Bathsheba. Who was it that David first sent to find out about her? Who were the messengers he later sent to get her? Did Joab really not know why David was asking him to send Uriah to the foremost part of the fighting where he was sure to be killed?

Why do spiritual leaders fall? Sometimes because their families and friends, who ought to step in and say something, keep silent and let them get away with murder.

But in talking about perhaps the most publicized fall of all time among spiritual leaders, we've gone too far. We were looking for "Secret Falls." What we learned along the way was that what we believe to be "secret sins" may not be so secret after all. Secret falls have a nasty way of growing so big that, before you know it, everyone is beating a path to see them. As God said to David through Nathan, referring to the calamity that would befall David, "You did it in secret, but I will do this thing in broad daylight before all Israel" (2 Samuel 12:12).

David's Secret Fall

To learn more about secret falls, we need to rewind the

tape to the point just before the whole nation knew what David had done. Run it back to the point where David got up from his bed and walked out to the roof of the palace. The first question is, What was David doing on the roof that night to begin with? And why did a man who already had not *one* but *many* wives feel compelled to have yet another woman for his pleasure? Was it because forbidden fruit seemed sweeter? Was there in this man of adventure a heightened sense of excitement when risk was involved?

Most curious of all, how could this consummate man of God abandon his values so quickly and so easily? My good friend Jim McGoldrick writes the most moving personal reflections on various characters and situations which he finds specially touching him through the Scriptures. At the conclusion to each of his poignant essays, Jim composes what I've come to think of as the unwritten prayers of the Bible. His comments about David, and the prayer which he imagines David might have prayed, are keenly intuitive and helpful to our understanding of secret falls. In the next few paragraphs, let me share with you Jim's rich insight about David's "secret" sin.

"Where was David, *the man of prayer*, when he stood on that rooftop and saw Bathsheba below? If anything is clear in the Bible, it is that David was a man of prayer. A man of prayer from his earliest dealings with King Saul and Saul's troubled mind. Time and time again, in moments of stress and moments of danger, David turned quickly to the Lord in prayer and saw his prayers answered. Even in the aftermath of David's being confronted about his sin with Bathsheba, David prayed for the unborn infant, fasted fervently, and begged God to change his mind and let the infant live.

"But on that rooftop, overlooking the city and seeing the beautiful Bathsheba below, where is that man of prayer? Was there no prayer that David might have offered that could have helped him fight the battles within his own mind—that could have led to a different result?

"What if David had offered a prayer something like this? Might it not have made a difference?

Father, I thought my battles were won. My enemies have fled before my armies as your mighty arm struck them down. But if I am so strong and mighty, why do I feel so small and alone; why do I toss and turn in my bed; why are my knees so weak as I return to this place night after night? Why does my desire rob me of my ability to sleep, to concentrate, to reason? Why do I keep returning to fuel these burning desires? My face is white-hot. I know it is wrong to want what I see; to want without counting the cost; to want what I know is so wrong because the feeling seems so right.

Lord, you have slain the man with the bow, the armored soldier in the chariot, the mercenaries lying in wait. Can you not let me know how a king must behave? Can I not recall that to abuse power is a sin against you and a betrayal of my people? Help me keep my moral force that I need to rule this unwieldy people. Give me the power to make good decisions; to exercise my power to reason, to let reason control; to let these desires die down; to love you and your ways; to be the man you want me to be; to keep your faith, the faith of my family; to be the husband, the father, the leader that only your power can let me be.

Now, give me the strength to will these feet, one in front of the other, back to my bed, alone, to sleep and not to dream.

> Give me your strength to defeat the enemies
> in my mind, just as you have the enemies on
> the field. And please, Lord, let me not dream.
> Let me not dream.

In focusing on David, the man in need of prayer, Jim has answered yet another question for us: Why do spiritual leaders find themselves in sin? Because they forget to do what they do best. After praying so ardently for others, they fail to pray for themselves.

Secret Guilt for Secret Sin

Secret falls are found in all our backyards. They just seem more out of place for recognized spiritual leaders. Yet perhaps spiritual leaders are all the more vulnerable. Like David, they have won more than their share of spiritual battles. Perhaps their guard is down when it counts most. Perhaps they fight so many spiritual battles—in the pulpit, in the intensive care wards, in the counseling sessions, in the many church meetings they must attend—that they are left weak and empty.

There is a sense in which David was fortunate. As embarrassing and disgraceful as it was when his sin became household news, at least he was relieved of the burden of living with his guilt. Remember how fervently he prayed and fasted for the child before it died; then, learning of the child's death, how he got up, washed himself, and ate? Because David's sin was made public, he was able to acknowledge it, pray for forgiveness, and then go on with his life in full confidence of God's mercy.

What concerns me are all those spiritual leaders who are eaten away with guilt for sins which are known only to themselves and God. Those worldly thoughts that keep penetrating their spiritual selves. Those carnal fantasies which sometimes play X-rated movies in their minds, perhaps at the very moment they are engaged in acts of worship. Those feelings of hatred, revenge, or bitterness toward someone they are supposed to be leading spiritually. The inability to forgive those who have trespassed against them.

Perhaps there was that time they got drunk while the family was away from home. Or the "adult" movie they watched at the hotel while attending a Christian conference. Perhaps the lie they told about being sick, when the truth is that they spent the week struggling over whether they could really believe in the inerrancy of the Bible. Or the very fact that they let themselves doubt at all. Perhaps there was an affair years ago. Or an affair they wish they could have. Maybe it's the foul language they use when they're not around other Christians. Maybe it's the time they hit their wife in anger.

"Physician, heal thyself." If you have encouraged others to be more faithful and pure, have you not taken time lately to encourage yourself? Have you used every excuse you can lay your hands on to justify sin in your life? Have you, like David, forgotten to pray for moral courage in the face of temptation?

On the other hand, if you have preached God's forgiveness for others, have you not believed it for yourself? Have you been harder on yourself than you believe God will be on those who look to you for leadership? Have you talked about grace as if it belonged to everyone but you? Would you prefer to wallow in guilt rather than muster the fortitude to truly repent and walk a higher road?

Well-known falls inevitably rob a spiritual leader of his ability to influence other people. We see it in David's case, where he failed to take any action against his son Amnon, after Amnon raped his own half-sister, Tamar. Nor was David able to act from a position of moral strength against his son Absalom, who killed Amnon in an ambush. After all, David himself had committed both a sexual sin and the sin of murder. Who was he to preach to others?

Secret falls can also have the same effect, particularly if the spiritual leader is truly conscientious about his ministry. If he has a moral weakness in a particular area, he may feel himself unworthy to preach or teach against other people participating in that very sin. He fears his own hypocrisy. And, of course, if he were to preach against it arrogantly and unsympathetically, he would indeed lay himself open to that charge. He has compromised his ability to censure others harshly.

However, as ugly as the sin is itself, ultimately there may be a way to use one's struggle with sin for the good of others. One's dark side can sometimes actually be a way to spiritual enlightenment—not that one ought to run out and foolishly enroll in "Dark Sides 101" as a freshman course in life.

Paul's Lesson from Temptation

Are you intrigued, as I am, with Paul's agonizing confession that even he—the apostle Paul—did things that he knew he shouldn't do? That he had battles with temptation and sin? Paul's great consciousness of sin may have been due more to a heightened *sensitivity* to sin than actual sin itself. But, however deep or shallow the depth of his sin, it clearly weighed heavily on his heart.

So how did whatever personal battles he may have referred to affect him as a spiritual leader? He certainly didn't seem to pull any punches regarding any particular sin. Whatever secret battles may have haunted his conscience, it didn't stop him from calling all sin "sin." To the contrary, whatever Paul's spiritual "thorns" might have been, they turned out to be roses which he shared with other people in his ministry. If weakness had made him sin, he says that he found strength in such weakness. With candor, Paul says that it was through his sinful self that he had come to know the grace of God.

If Paul's letters to the Romans, Ephesians, and Galatians contain the most brilliant exposition of God's grace in all of Scripture, was it not surely because he was drawing from a wellspring of understanding gained from his own spiritual struggles?

Turning Weakness into Strength

I think I can relate to Paul's tie between personal weakness and the strength of one's ministry to others. As I came through school I was usually on top of the pile, or close to it. In high school I was Big Man on Campus: Student Body President, champion debater, voted "Most Intellectual," and other such silliness. In college I continued to think pretty highly of myself, academically and otherwise. But in my first semester in law school I nearly flunked out. It may have had something to do with the fact that I was working almost full-time and was feeling the depression of having lost the love of my life. But it happened nevertheless. And it was a devastating blow to my ego, from which I've never recovered. Fortunately.

Somewhat like Paul, I have been able to use my academic weakness to strengthen others. Somehow along the way I fooled somebody and became a law professor myself. It's funny how things turn around. Now, when anxious students come into my office worried to death about their grades, I lower my voice and tell them my story. So far there haven't been many whose first-semester averages were less than mine! With their usual inflated estimation of the faculty's brilliance, they can hardly believe it. But it usually puts a smile on their face, and gives them a new determination to outdo their ol' Criminal Law prof!

I also know this feeling of weakness-turned-to-strength on the spiritual side of the ledger. Forget what my mother and sisters would tell you about what a sarcastic, bigheaded, and disrespectful kid I was growing up. It may be true, but let's say it wasn't. At my worst I was never the typical, wild "preacher's kid." Even through my college years, I hadn't smoked, taken a drink, cussed, or messed around. All in all, I was a pretty righteous guy. At least I *felt* righteous.

During my last year or so of law school, I was preaching regularly for a little congregation about 50 miles away. And even when I was a District Attorney in eastern Oregon, I did much of the preaching for the church I attended.

It was during that time in eastern Oregon that I first experienced what I recognized to be serious moral failure. If you've ever been to desertlike Malheur County, you can understand why I think of that period of my life as a kind of wilderness wandering. If in the eyes of the world what I did would be pretty tame stuff, as a Christian I knew it was sin—plain and simple—and it was devastating. Unable to preach to others, knowing what a sinner I was, I stepped down from the pulpit. It was the first time in my young adult life that I consciously thought of myself as unrighteous. And I've never quite recovered. Again, fortunately.

The truth is, of course, that I was unrighteous all along, even when I didn't think of myself that way. There were always sins of the heart and sins of the mind. But it was good for me to discover my own weakness, for, like Paul, I needed to learn about God's grace. I had come from a legalistic background (which, I must say, has more merit than most people think), but it was time to learn about the other side of God. Unfortunately, it took getting acquainted with sin to discover that side of him.

I don't mean to build a case for intentional sinning so that grace may abound all the more. Paul exploded that self-serving rationalization long ago (Romans 6:1,2). But in fact I've been closer to God in my heart ever since I first seriously acknowledged my sinfulness. And I've been a far more effective Christian communicator as well. Before my secret fall I couldn't really understand people who struggled with sin. Now at last I understood. When I finally started preaching again, my sermons were different. They were more personal, more confessional, more practical, more loving.

Spiritual failure need not be a total loss. God can take our rubbish and recycle it into exquisite gifts for others.

Surprise Secret Sin

Have you read Psalm 90 recently? Verse 12, "Teach us to number our days aright, that we may gain a heart of wisdom," is one of my favorite passages. And the psalm sounds so typical of David—particularly when the writer says, "You have set our iniquities before you, our *secret sins* in the light of your presence." Was David referring here to his sin with Bathsheba before it was made public?

If you don't already know, you're in for a surprise. Our supersinner, David, was not even the author of Psalm 90. The heading of the psalm attributes the prayer to "Moses the man of God."

As a lawyer, when I think of Moses, I think of him as the great lawgiver. Of course, the laws of Moses were *God's* laws; Moses didn't think them up himself. Yet because Moses was so instrumental in bringing the nation of Israel out of Egypt and forming them into a nation for God's own possession, he had an intimacy with God that permitted him an invitation into the very presence of the Holy One! It makes it all the harder to believe that Moses would have disappointed God at the waters of Meribah. We all should be so fortunate as to be the man of God that Moses was. Despite Moses' sin at the rock of Meribah, God later greatly honored him on the Mount of Transfiguration.

But there it is in black and white in the 90th psalm—an admission by the great spiritual leader, Moses, that he too struggled with secret sin. There was more in his life than his much-publicized fall. There were secret falls as well. Were they falls of faith, when perhaps he doubted whether God would actually provide the promised land? Were they falls of attitude, when perhaps he wished disaster would overtake those who opposed his leadership?

We will never know, of course, but we can surely appreciate that, like us, Moses had secret sin. Yet Moses persevered, whatever his private misgivings about his guilt before God. Keenly aware of his mortality, he sought a heart of wisdom. Perhaps at times God gave him that wisdom through the most unlikely avenue of all—Moses' own secret sin.

With the consummately righteous Moses as our example, perhaps there are times when God also gives *us* wisdom through our secret sins as well. Are we floundering in guilt and self-defeat, or are we open to God transforming our brokenness into lives of service for others? Are we content to continue in our secret sin, or are we, like Moses, ready to hand over our self-will in exchange for God's guidance?

If nothing else, our sin reminds us that whatever spiritual leadership we may exercise—whether formally or informally—it is *God's* leadership, not our own. Moses was well aware of that. He closes his psalm with a prayer that should be on the lips of each of us:

> May the favor of the Lord our God rest upon us;
> establish the work of our hands for us—
> yes, establish the work of our hands.

Happy Endings for Secret Sins

Secret falls can easily erode our lives and the lives of those around us, to no one's benefit. We must avoid them at all cost. If caught up in secret sin, we need forgiveness—no matter who we are or how important we think we may be in the kingdom. But if we channel them properly, God can use even our spiritual falls to lift others up. Moses fell, not only at Meribah in the presence of his people, but secretly in the presence of God. Yet just as the water from the rock of his public sin refreshed a thirsty people in the wilderness, so too the lessons he learned from his unrecorded sins have encouraged every person familiar with his life of faith and service before God.

It's just as well that secret falls are not seen. They're never pretty. But the water that flows out of them, when filtered through true repentance and God's forgiving mercy, can end up being some of the most refreshing of all to a world thirsting for spiritual life.

Looking Within

- Is it possible that you have let imagined fears about your qualifications to lead others rob you of opportunities for fruitfulness in the Lord's work?
- Do you measure your value to God more in terms of results or of efforts?
- Is someone close to you risking his or her ability to lead others? Is there a way you can prevent this from happening?
- Have you called a truce in your own struggle with sin, or do you continue to seriously wage a battle with temptation and immorality?
- If you have succumbed to some humiliating sin in your life, have you given up on yourself, or have you used your weakness to strengthen others?

5

Hidden Falls

Strength Through Sharing the Struggles

My analogy between waterfalls and spiritual falls can be misleading if we're not careful. When we think of waterfalls, most of us think of something beautiful to watch. And if those are the only waterfalls we can think of, then they won't come close to describing a spiritual fall. Spiritual falls are anything but beautiful. They are ugly.

I have seen many beautiful waterfalls with pure water flowing over rocky precipices, dropping with elegance and grace to the valley floor below. But I have also stood on a steel bridge over the Iguazú Falls in South America, with the roar of churning, dirty, chocolate-colored waters from a late spring runoff beneath me, and felt power like a thousand jet engines revved to maximum capacity. I later read that other tourists at the same spot were swept to their deaths when the force of the water ripped the bridge from its moorings.

When we harbor imaginary falls in our minds, or encounter secret sins which only we and God know about, that is disaster enough. But when our sins are open to other people, and when others are affected by our sins, there is destruction, not enjoyment. There is ugliness, not beauty. There is death, not life. The falls are not fun anymore. The tourists have been swept to their deaths. They have drowned in swirling, muddy waters of sin. They have families that will never again know peace in their lives. They have unfinished projects that will never be completed. They have hopes and aspirations lying in broken heaps at the bottom of the falls.

What we want to talk about in this chapter are all those polluted and deadly falls we hope never to see. The ones with the signs reading: "Warning! Water Not Fit for Human Consumption." "Warning! Risk of Death Beyond this Point." These are the falls where destruction has come because warning signs were ignored.

But instead of concentrating on salvage operations, where all we can do is pick up the pieces and put them into a box for shipping home, I want us to look at the possibilities of rescue operations, where precious souls can be nurtured and brought back into useful service for the Lord.

No Man Is an Island

The older I get, the more I value the sharing of simple things with others—special others. I used to travel around the world for three months at a time, with just a little canvass bag as my companion. I saw the great wonders of the far-flung continents. If no one was around at the time, it hardly bothered me. I just drank it all in anyway. If other tourists were nearby, sometimes I would make friends and share the moment with them.

But these days it's harder to look at a sunset, or a quaint country village, or a newborn lamb in the field, without wanting to share it with someone else. Sometimes I turn around to say, "Look," only to catch myself with the reality that I am standing there alone.

I don't mean to moan. It's just that good times are always better when they're shared. And for the most part, bad times too. Of course when bad times involve sin, it's a bad time we probably prefer just went away. Certainly we would not wish for other people to know we have failed. But when they already *do* know, then our fall can turn out better than we might expect if it is shared, and shared properly.

Private Falls

On our trek through the treacherous terrain of spiritual leadership, we are likely to run across one or more "Private Falls." We encounter them when there are other people who know about our sin, but who minister to us in our hour of need. They understand. They care. They are sensitive to our reputations. They may rebuke and they may scold, but they love us dearly. And they stick with us when others won't. They pray with us and encourage us. They keep in touch. If there were glorious sunsets, they would happily share them with us. But even if we experience storm clouds and rain, they will share that too.

It only takes a major scandal in the Christian community to fully appreciate how different it might be if, instead of wanting to keep your fall private, someone jumped at the chance to expose you. When revenge, political jockeying, and personal vendettas are the order of the day, "Private Falls" can all too easily be renamed "Public Falls." But it needn't happen. It's not God's way.

Why do spiritual leaders fall—over and over sometimes? Because there is no one there to help them on the comeback trail. And because, instead of love and caring, all they find is hostility and avoidance.

The Beauty of Private Concern

That godly couple Aquila and Priscilla set the proper tone for us in a situation involving not sin as such but doctrinal error—or, perhaps better stated, doctrinal misunderstanding. When it was obvious that the scholarly and zealous Apollos knew only about the baptism of John, Aquila and Priscilla recognized his need to learn more about Jesus and about baptism into his name.

If many of us had been in their shoes, we would have challenged Apollos to a public debate, or written scathing articles about him in some church newspaper. Maybe we would have even gone on radio or television to point out how wrong he was. But you know the story. Aquila and Priscilla "invited him to their home and explained to him the way of God more adequately" (Acts 18:26). There was no need for a public spectacle, no need to humiliate this sincere man of God.

One can only shudder at the thought of what might have happened to Apollos' ministry had Aquila and Priscilla not come to him privately and in a spirit of love. Apollos might have reacted defensively and turned away from the truth. Others might have been persuaded to mark Apollos for life as a heretic. Like many spiritual leaders, Apollos might have been so embarrassed and discouraged by public rebuke that he could have abandoned his ministry altogether. What a loss to the kingdom that would have been!

Private Restorations

When actual sin is involved, the situation changes, but only slightly. There is still the need for love and for confidentiality, as far as it can be maintained. Whatever else might be called for in a given situation, Paul urged mutual responsibility and self-examination in the restoration of a fallen brother or sister:

> Brothers, if someone is caught in a sin, you who are spiritual should restore him gently. But watch yourself, or you also may be tempted. Carry each other's burdens, and in this way you will fulfill the law of Christ (Galatians 6:1,2).

Three things stand out. First, those who attempt to restore the fallen one are wearing a fairly presumptuous label: "you who are spiritual." Just in case the wrong kind of people volunteer for the restoration squad, Paul hastens to add:

> If anyone thinks he is something when he is nothing, he deceives himself. Each one should test his own actions. Then he can take pride in himself, without comparing himself to some-body else, for each one should carry his own load (Galatians 6:3-5).

Unless we are careful, we may assume wrongfully that we are the truly spiritual ones when in fact we are not. The issue is probably best determined by the speed with which we jump to the task of setting another person straight. If we can't wait to do it, we're probably the wrong ones to do it. If, on the other hand, we proceed only with the greatest reluctance, we may be just the ones best fit for the job.

Second, we are to approach the fallen person only while holding a mirror in our hand—pointed toward ourselves! It's a sobering thought, isn't it? Who among us is ever really in a position to censure anybody else, particularly someone who has been a faithful spiritual leader? But this self-scrutiny is important if we are to satisfy the third requirement—that we restore him gently. One who has his own sinfulness uppermost in mind can hardly be insensitive to a fellow sinner.

We understand gentle restoration when we take pains to lovingly restore an antique. We don't use a belt sander when light rubbing with fine sandpaper will do. Nor do we sand against the grain, for it will leave scars we can never get out. And never would we slap on a coat of paint just to cover up the imperfections. It's the imperfections which give the wood character and warmth. We stain it to enhance the beauty despite its wear and tear—but only as much as it can take without detracting from the original.

If we would take this much care with a broken piece of furniture, why would we even consider taking less care with a broken brother or sister in Christ?

Does this mean that we are to maintain privacy, where possible, about such sensational sins as sexual immorality and drunkenness? Are they not more serious than the garden-variety mental sins of hatred, discord, jealousy, selfish ambition, dissensions, and envy? Paul didn't seem to make any distinction when, in Galatians 5:19-21, he listed them all as "acts of the sinful nature."

If we are to learn anything from this passage, surely it is that Paul was trying to eliminate the haste with which we attempt to destroy one another. The thrust of Paul's letter to the Galatians is that in Christ we are free—free, that is, to serve one another in love. Those who would unnecessarily destroy a brother or sister in Christ may find it coming back at them. It was Paul who said it first: "If you keep on biting and devouring each other, watch out or you will be destroyed by each other" (Galatians 5:15). There is at least one well-known preacher who undoubtedly could tell us something about how that works.

A Bridge Over Private Falls

So when we do discover private falls, how are we to proceed? Is there an approach we should use? That concern is addressed by Jesus himself. "If your brother sins against you," Jesus counseled, "go and show him his fault, just between the two of you. If he listens to you, you have won your brother over" (Matthew 18:15). Contrary to what we are usually told, Jesus says that we *should* take it personally when someone offends us. That is, we should take the matter *personally* and *privately* to the one who has offended us, and do our best to work it out.

The wisdom is obvious: The more people who are

involved, the more pride that is at stake; and the more pride that is at stake, the less chance of resolving the problem.

Although in this passage Jesus was not directly addressing the issue of what we are to do when the fall of a spiritual leader is known by only one or perhaps a few others within his circle of influence, surely the principles are the same. Relatively private sins by spiritual leaders should not be treated any differently from the private sins of other people. Only the most insensitive person could overlook such a good opportunity for the loving restoration of a broken leader. And who deserves it more than one who has given so much of himself in the pursuit of restoring others?

Naturally, the assumption is that we are dealing with a conscientious, if weakened, spiritual leader. If that is not the case, then we will likely encounter a negative reaction for all our efforts. In such event, Jesus' teaching continues to point the direction:

> But if he will not listen, take one or two others along, so that "every matter may be established by the testimony of two or three witnesses." If he refuses to listen to them, tell it to the church; and if he refuses to listen even to the church, treat him as you would a pagan or a tax collector (Matthew 18:16,17).

If a spiritual leader does not respond positively to our efforts to keep his fall private, then he forces us to go public. One's attitude toward his sin may make all the difference between whether the sign reads "Private Falls" or "Public Falls." Yet, even in this, our own attitude toward restoration may affect the attitude we receive in response. Love begets love, and understanding encourages true repentance.

Sharing in the Triumph

When I look back on "Private Falls," the spray and mist get into my eyes. At least, I think it's mist. Or maybe it's tears of defeat, embarrassment, and shame. But there are also tears of joy, for those who cared enough to share it with me. For those who believed in me and in what I could become. For those who forgave me. For those who lifted me higher. They have given me a second chance to serve the Lord. And in whatever feeble way I might do that, *my* successes are *their* successes. They participate in my ministry, for those who share another person's gloom are a part of all his tomorrows.

"Private Falls" are not places we want to go for a picnic. They are not waters we want to get anywhere near. They are polluted, discolored, and destructive. But when one of us has strayed in that direction, ignored all the warning signs, and fallen to our own destruction, even polluted "Private Falls" can be a place where those who love each other can meet. A lot of people would prefer "Public Falls" because they are bigger and more spectacular. But you find little love there.

Is there a broken figure calling to us from the bottom of "Private Falls"? Are we willing to overcome the stench and deadly roar in order to rescue him? Who knows—someday it could be us at the bottom.

Blackmail Falls

When a spiritual leader falls, there is usually someone there to catch him—a spouse, a friend, or perhaps another spiritual leader. But sometimes when a spiritual leader falls, there is someone there to catch him . . . in the act. The *very* act, if possible! There are falls which on the surface look every bit like "Private Falls" but couldn't be more different. Their waters are not only polluted but bitter. You won't find a drop of love or concern in these falls, because they are the outrageous and dreaded "Blackmail Falls." In these falls someone has intentionally poisoned the water.

In "Blackmail Falls" the spiritual leader's sins are not made public, but are held over his head by someone who wants to take advantage of the leader's sin for his own gain. In the extreme case, normally involving only big-name leaders, hush money may be demanded and paid. Of course, there are those who could tell us that hush money has no guarantees attached. In fact, when the private fall inevitably becomes public, the news about the payment of hush money simply compounds the crime. If he wasn't guilty, the public questions, why did he agree to pay?

In other cases there may be political motives or other personal advantages to be gained. Confrontation regarding one's sin comes in the context of whatever other concerns there may be. If it is some favored position that the blackmailer wants to assure, the many "advantages" of securing or maintaining that position are made clear. If it is support for a pet project or cause that one has in mind, he intimates with calculated force the many "benefits" of receiving that support. Among the "advantages" and "benefits," of course, is the tacit agreement that the spiritual leader's sin will not end up in "Scandal Falls." If the fallen man of God cooperates, his reputation will remain untarnished.

When the Other Shoe Drops

If you are a spiritual leader, have I touched a sensitive nerve? Does this scenario sound agonizingly familiar to you? Have you seen more than you ever wanted to see of "Blackmail Falls"? If so, undoubtedly you have been called on to make some pretty difficult decisions.

How did you handle it? Did you talk about it with anyone? Did you have the courage to call your accuser's bluff, or have you yielded to his pressure and given him what he wanted? Has your entire ministry been compromised, or only certain aspects? Have you been able to forgive whoever has done this to you? Have you been able to forgive *yourself* for ever letting yourself become vulnerable?

The Scriptures don't have much to say about this unusual situation, but there is a vitally important proverb about bribery, which could also describe what takes place in blackmail: "A wicked man accepts a bribe in secret to pervert the course of justice" (Proverbs 17:23). It could be said that compromising one's integrity at the risk of being exposed is tantamount to giving a bribe. At all cost, certainly, one ought to avoid turning over his conscience to another person, particularly one whose ulterior motives are far from pure.

Overcoming the Bitterness

It would be hard to imagine anyone more entitled to feelings of hatred and revenge than one who lives each day under the threat of exposure at someone else's whim. Yet once again the Proverbs give us this wisdom: "Do not say, 'I'll pay you back for this wrong!' Wait for the Lord, and he will deliver you" (Proverbs 20:22). The advice is as practical as it is godly. There are those today who undoubtedly wish they had followed that advice more closely.

I suspect that, rather than revenge, the bigger problem for the victims of "Blackmail Falls" is forgiveness. Forgiveness is easier when a wrong is done and over with. Harmony comes from confession, prayer, and resolution of the sin. But extortion is a continuing offense. There's no end to it. As a result, forgiveness can be most difficult. But it has to be done or else it will eat away at a fallen leader until he is consumed by it. Dealing with the guilt of the sin would be difficult enough, but adding the sin of unforgiveness would be more than most people could bear.

Therefore, as with all situations where forgiveness is difficult, *agape* love involves *acting* as if you love the person even when you don't. As William Glasser (*Reality Therapy*) put it: "It's easier to act your way to a better way of feeling than it is to feel your way to a better way of acting." Who knows? If we act lovingly toward those who have taken wrongful advantage of us, we may one day pierce through their malicious hearts and find a heart of love. And, best of all, we can lift our own heads high without the shame they have attempted to heap upon us. Certainly if Jesus could forgive the one who betrayed him, so also should we.

It is almost unbelievable that there would be "Blackmail Falls" hidden anywhere near the Christian community. But we've already been witness to fairly prominent public ones in our midst. So it is likely that there are many more out there, hidden beneath the surface.

God forgive those who, for their own selfish gain, would compromise the ministry of struggling, fallible, spiritual leaders. God forgive all of us spiritual leaders who have compromised our own ministries by giving them an open door.

All for One, One for All

"Imagination Falls," "Secret Falls," "Private Falls," and "Blackmail Falls"—these are the silent and hidden falls of spiritual leaders all around us. We don't see them right away, plainly signposted, as we have done in this chapter. But if we look closely we may see evidence of them. There may be a less strident tone in one's preaching, or perhaps discouragement and alienation in the life of an elder or a deacon. The Bible class teacher may not provide as thorough coverage of certain subjects as he normally might.

Naturally, we should not jump to conclusions and assume we have discovered a silent fall when there could be any number of other explanations. But we should open ourselves to the possibility that our leaders are themselves struggling with temptation and sin behind the scenes. In fact, we can almost count on it.

When we think of the work of the church, we almost always focus on those who are part of the "official" ministry. We comfortably cite the fact that Christ "gave some to be apostles, some to be prophets, some to be evangelists, and some to be pastors and teachers," and often fail to recognize our own responsibilities in the ending of the sentence—"to prepare God's people for works of service" (Ephesians 4:11,12).

Paul was writing to *all* the Christians in Ephesus about the mutual support which ought to come through the body life of the church as it looks to Christ, its head. "From him," Paul wrote, "the whole body, joined and held together by every supporting ligament, grows and builds itself up in love, as each part does its work" (Ephesians 4:16).

If spiritual leaders in the church are called to lead, the rest of us are called to give them whatever support they may need.

Lifting Up Holy Hands

I can't help but think of the Israelite's battle with the Amalekites. Moses had told Joshua and his troops that he would stand on top of the hill with the staff of God in his hands. There follows this account of how the Israelites won the battle:

> Joshua fought the Amalekites as Moses had ordered, and Moses, Aaron and Hur went to the top of the hill. As long as Moses held up his hands, the Israelites were winning, but whenever he lowered his hands, the Amalekites

were winning. When Moses' hands grew tired, they took a stone and put it under him and he sat on it. Aaron and Hur held his hands up— one on one side, one on the other—so that his hands remained steady till sunset. So Joshua overcame the Amalekite army with the sword (Exodus 17:10-13).

Who won the battle that day? Joshua, the great military general? Moses, the nation's political leader? All the brave soldiers who gave their lives along the fierce battle-front?

Were it not for the inspiration of Scripture, we might never have known about the seemingly insignificant role of Aaron and Hur. They weren't on the front line, where the clash of swords could mean death with the next thrust. Nor were they in charge of strategy or logistics. All they had to do was to help Moses keep his hands lifted. That didn't take much skill, training, or particular courage. All it took was recognition of a need and the willingness to do what they could in support of a weakened leader.

What a difference we might see in the church if there were more Christians aware of the silent and hidden falls of their spiritual leaders! If there were more prayers on their behalf, more understanding of their doubts and discouragement. More appreciation of their struggles to be people of God, people of prayer, and people of strength on our behalf.

Looking Within

- Do you ever find yourself putting an acceptable gloss on sins in your life? Have you made ugly and destructive habits respectable?
- When you see your friends caught up in sin, do you ever confront them lovingly about it, or do you let it slide?

- When you see people you don't like caught up in sin, do you want to help them or would you rather expose their sin for all to see?
- Is there anyone who lives in constant fear that you might bring him disgrace? If so, might not this be a good time to resolve that issue forever?
- In what ways can you "hold up the hands" of those to whom you look for spiritual leadership?

6

The Trouble
with Second-Best

How the Church Courts Disaster

It's Sunday morning in the quiet Cotswold village of Buckland, England, where I've recently become a part-time resident. The 20 or so brown stone cottages scattered along the country lane, with its winding, babbling brook, present a postcard picture for the hikers who pass through while walking along the Cotswold Way. At the Buckland Manor Country House in the middle of the village, it will soon be time for Sunday lunch.

Out on the hillside it's lambing time for the sheep. The hand-scrawled sign on the steps over the fence reads "Lambs. Please keep dogs on lead." And the weekend equestrians are out in force, hunting good adventure, if not foxes, today. The locals, who love their dogs, are taking them for a walk down the lane, and the occasional tourist stops by the unmistakably-British red phone box to place a quick call.

As the time for morning worship arrives at the village church, only a handful of the faithful—two dozen or less—will show up for the service. Holy Communion will be observed in the prayer-book fashion of the Anglican Church, before the vicar apologizes for leaving hurriedly to preside over another service in the next village. Dwindling church attendance has divided his duties among five churches these days.

Only last year the longtime local rector resigned... under fire. After years of general discontent among the parishioners, the good rector was first hauled before an ecclesiastical jury and then himself appealed to the highest church court in England, the Court of Arches, as its first case in over 200 years. Talk about a fallen spiritual leader! The verdict? Guilty. The charge? Writing rude letters to parishioners! Seven other equally serious charges were dismissed.

The village was not unfamiliar with religious scandal. It seems that, some years ago, the local Temperance Band was disbanded after its members were discovered circling a haystack in the field, thinking it was a house. Apparently they had been doing some personal research into the evils of intemperance!

As elsewhere in England, the local villagers are quite proud of their church and its rich history. They're quick to point out that the earliest parts of the church date back to the thirteenth century, though naturally it has been renovated many times in the centuries since then. On occasion the great John Wesley preached in the Buckland church while he was visiting friends in the area.

Whenever I am asked what I'm doing in England and respond that I'm a writer, inevitably eyes light up. When they press further and learn that it's religious writing I do, a look of disappointment usually crosses their faces. They would hope for novels—or perhaps books on gardening. But to show interest in my subjects they invariably ask if I have visited the local church. "Our church has the most beautiful windows," says one. "It's the loveliest church in Gloucestershire," says another.

I'm sure I must distress them terribly when I tell them that back where I'm from when we talk about "the church" we are talking about the congregation. Of course I keep wondering if I'm right about that. I'm so used to being part of a fellowship which has no building of its own that I forget how much importance other Christians *do* attach to church buildings.

The great abbey at Tewkesbury is not far from me. It is a magnificent structure, but more the object of tourist

curiosity than the center for widespread spiritual interest among the residents of Tewkesbury. Personally, I
prefer to walk across the street and spend a few minutes
in silence in the Old Baptist Chapel, which was built in
1623, complete with a stone-lined baptistry in the floor.
There, in the shadow of the established church, courageous men and women of faith defied tradition and
personal scorn to worship God simply and humbly in a
back-alley meeting hall.

Over the past decade hundreds of chapels, rectories,
and church buildings in England have been deserted and
sold. Recently while looking for a cottage, I saw many of
these buildings converted into homes. Part of me wanted
to live in a converted chapel, thinking it would be an
appropriate place to write religious books. Another part
of me refused to be an accessory to the spiritual decline
in England. Everywhere you turn, you see former churches
now converted not only into homes but also into ware-
houses, shops, and even physical-fitness centers.

It makes me want to plaster the countryside with signs
saying "Convert *People*, Not Churches!" If the church as
a spiritual body were meeting the spiritual needs of its
people, then it would be *building* buildings, not convert-
ing them to lesser uses.

Even in what churches remain, few visitors will ever
have trouble finding a vacant seat. Evensong in larger
cathedrals or abbeys is usually so poorly attended that
those who do come are likely to sit with the choir. Naturally, church attendance is not the essence of one's
relationship with God, but it can be an embarrassing
barometer of community interest in spirituality.

It is sad to see a "Christian nation" whose primary ties
to God are stained glass, official ritual, and overworn
tradition. What relatively few active believers remain
might say I've overstated the case, but most of them
would readily admit that the church as an institution is

on a downhill slide. Even some of the church leaders I've talked to behind closed doors have admitted that the church has lost sight of its mission. As a result, it is not surprising to hear a person on the street confide: "The Church of England is Christianity's own worst enemy."

Of course, it is not only the Church of England whose buildings are being sold off for condo conversions. The Methodists, Baptists, Congregationalists, and other fellowships are feeling the same pinch. But it is the Church of England which is the official state church. It is the Church of England which is primarily responsible for the education of England's young people. It is the Church of England which controls religious broadcasting on radio and television, and sets the religious tone in this country. Therefore it is the Church of England which must bear most of the responsibility for what may be one of the least spiritual "Christian nations" on earth. This same church, whose men and women of faith have given us thousands of inspiring hymns, has now found itself in almost total eclipse.

An Object Lesson

In the event you think I have forgotten which book I am writing, there is a point to all of this. In the first century the church of Jesus Christ had no buildings, no stained glass, no ritual, no tradition, no clergy, no ecclesiastical hierarchy, no official status, no educational system, no control over public avenues of communication, and no broad-based financial support. Yet it conquered the world! Today the Church of England has all those things, and it's dying a slow and horrible death. Surely this is more than coincidence.

Nor can the decline be explained away with such excuses as "cultural slide" or "changing times." The Church of England was already moribund in the time of Charles Darwin, who came close to becoming a local church rector at a time when he said he had no idea what he even believed. In his day, if young men of aristocracy had no ability to succeed in law or medicine, their fathers saw to it that they acquired a respectable position in the church. For more than a century the Anglican Church has been comfortably maintained by a caretaker clergy.

Peter Brent, Darwin's sympathetic biographer, described the languid church as it existed even in the 1800's:

> All over the English countryside, the Church spread somnolently in its unpretentious patchwork of parishes, maintained by scattered regiments of vicars, rectors, parsons and curates. These, making up in stamina for what they lacked in energy, fitted into their little districts as snugly as the churchyard yew-trees, smiling at babies and droning from pulpits for decade after comfortable decade. They were the props and adjuncts—and, frequently, the offspring—of the gentry and the aristocracy, by whom they had in many cases been appointed. In their gentlemanly, apathetic hands Christianity sagged, faded and shredded like the ancient banners that adorned their churches. The fact that the clerical profession was often chosen as the last resort of the family dullard did nothing to lead to a revival (*Charles Darwin*, Hamlyn Publishing, pp. 71-72).

Why do some spiritual leaders fall? It could be because they are in positions of leadership for all the wrong reasons.

And who could have imagined the negative impact on faith in England when the church fully embraced Darwin's rejection of divine creation! When church leaders buried the body of Charles Darwin with full honors in Westminster Abbey they also buried any chance they might have for spiritual credibility in a nation already choking from institutional Christianity.

When spiritual leaders have abandoned the teachings of the Word which they have been called to proclaim, it should come as no surprise that their influence has been destroyed.

But there is an even more important lesson to be learned from the Anglican experience. Wake up for this one, and let it send chills through your soul with all the force of a ship's horn furiously blasting into the night a warning of fire on board. Through the dramatic demise of the Anglican Church we are confronted graphically and compellingly with the horrible possibility of what can happen to a whole nation of church leaders and to those who have followed them: An entire church can fall!

Not that it should come as any surprise. The entire nation of Israel fell when its spiritual leaders led them astray. And when the fall came, it was not just the leaders who suffered; the entire nation suffered. But think of it—an entire church brought to its knees for failure of courageous and biblical spiritual leadership. Are we to think that we are somehow immune here in America?

Opting for Second-Best

A second lesson to be learned from the Anglican experience is that spiritual leaders are often the products of the churches and organizations of which they are a part. If the church itself is not what it ought to be, can its leaders be what *they* ought to be? If the church is scandalized, can its leaders escape unscathed? And if the church and its leaders have departed from the biblical pattern, can the rest of us possibly be unaffected? Before we answer those questions more fully, permit me another brief detour.

A friend of mine recently made an interesting observation. "Have you ever considered," he asked, "that God sometimes accepts second-best, but that second-best will always run into problems?" As an example of what he meant, he referred to God's reluctant willingness to give Israel a king. The people of Israel were not satisfied with the God of all Creation being their sovereign Ruler. They had to have a king, like the nations around them. I suspect that what they really wanted was the pomp and circumstance associated with royalty. (When I am in England, I am acutely aware of that apparent need.) Some of them probably asked sincerely, "How are you supposed to pay homage to someone you can't even see?"

Like a father reluctantly allowing his teenager to discover for herself the pitfalls of what she foolishly insists on doing, God permitted Israel to have kings. But with what disastrous results for the nation! Yes, God had allowed what was second-best, but Israel paid a high price through the calamities which befell it, culminating in the nation's complete destruction.

Another example of the principle of second-best and the problems which accompany it is the practice of polygamy. God never specifically authorized it through Scripture, but he apparently permitted the practice of polygamy through the time of David and Solomon. One can only speculate why, but it is more than clear that it brought untold problems. We don't have to look much further than the hatred between Sarah and Hagar, or the childbearing competition between Rachel and Leah. As early as the Mosaic instructions regarding kings is found this warning: "He must not take many wives, or his heart will be led astray" (Deuteronomy 17:17). It should not be surprising, then, that this epitaph was written about King Solomon: "He had seven hundred wives of royal birth and three hundred concubines, and his wives led him astray" (1 Kings 11:3).

We see the principle of second-best once again when Jesus suggested that the certificate of divorce permitted under the Laws of Moses was only a concession. Again, one can only speculate as to why it was permitted, but Jesus makes it clear that divorce was never God's perfect will. And need we rehearse the litany of problems which accompany divorce? Clearly second-best never escapes unscathed.

If you are still wondering what possible tie there could be between the Church of England, the principle of second-best, and a book on fallen spiritual leaders, we can now assemble the seemingly unrelated pieces. Why is the Church of England reeling on the ropes, dazed and bloodied? Because it has allowed itself to lapse into an institutional malaise which, at best, is second-best. It is second-best because it has all the trappings of a church but little of its soul. It is second-best because it has a rich history, going back for centuries, but not far enough back to recapture the vibrancy of the first-century church. It is second-best because it has stained-glass churches, but can't fill them with bloodstained believers.

Second-best looks like it ought to work, but it never does. Second-best feels warm and comfortable, but it leaves us cold and unfulfilled. If we settle for second-best, we will never be truly satisfied. If we settle for second-best, we're bound to fail somewhere along the line.

The Church of England is not a force to be reckoned with in America. Few of us are even familiar with Anglican doctrine or practice. Although more and more Anglican congregations are discovering a back-to-the-Bible evangelicalism, American evangelicals would have little kinship with the traditional Church of England. So it is easy—perhaps too easy—for us to criticize unknown Anglicans across the Atlantic.

My aim in referring to the Church of England certainly has not been to assault it gratuitously. I have great love and appreciation for those who are doing all they can do to turn the church around, and for those stalwarts of faith who doggedly keep open what few doors remain standing. If I disagree with their doctrine, I nevertheless applaud their zeal. It's not at all the Anglicans that I'm centrally concerned about in this book. Rather, it is the Christian community in America that worries me.

We too have accepted second-best. The Anglicans themselves could take legitimate potshots at mainstream evangelicals. If Anglicans are further down the road toward disaster, we are well on our way. In fact, there are any number of ways in which we make the Church of England look good. So far they have been spared our garish Christian commercialism, and our side-show-like presentations of the gospel. If Anglican leaders wrongly resist the use of public television for anything likely to be interpreted as active evangelism, at least British television is devoid of money-centered ministries which spend as much time begging for "love gifts" as in spreading the Word. Yes, we too have settled for second-best.

Suffering Because of Second-Best

When we see the entire Christian community maligned by the fall of widely recognized spiritual leaders, it is time for some serious introspection. It's too easy for some to suggest that, as it turned out, they weren't spiritual men after all—that they were only masquerading as men of God when all along they were spiritual frauds. It's also too easy for others to suggest that what any spiritual leader might do to disgrace himself should not cause such an uproar within the church, that we should let the secular press have its field day snickering at Christianity, and then get on with our lives.

No, it is much deeper than that. I'm even foolish enough to think that the current climate of scandal could be a blessing in disguise if it can spur us on to think about how the church itself bears much of the responsibility for what has happened.

It will be an unfair comparison, which I trust no one will quote out of context. But we know that Adolf Hitler did not rise to power on his own shoestrings. Along the way he had to receive widespread public support. Likewise, without widespread public support a superstar televangelist doesn't rise to such a position of prominence that his fall can give a black eye to the entire Christian community. The question is, Was that widespread public support warranted? Does that notoriety itself lead to one's fall?

I have no interest in doing a postmortem autopsy on any big-name preacher who has fallen. By this time each of us will have drawn our own conclusions. The bigger picture is far more important. And what I'm afraid I see in the big picture is a far cry from New Testament Christianity. What I think I see is a Christian community that has suffered because—like the Church of England, and in only slightly different ways—it has accepted second-best.

An Ironic Flashback

The irony is that we may have succumbed to the same problems which destroyed Israel when they insisted on being ruled by kings. If we are honest with ourselves, we may be able to see our own situation described in the rules which God laid down for kings. We find those rules, amazingly enough, in the laws of Moses, instituted long before Israel's first king ever took the throne. As if anticipating the problems which would arise under a king, God said through Moses:

> When you enter the land the Lord your God
> is giving you and have taken possession of it
> and settled in it, and you say, "Let us set a king
> over us like all the nations around us," be sure

to appoint over you the king the Lord your God chooses. . . .

The king, moreover, must not acquire great numbers of horses for himself. . . . He must not accumulate large amounts of silver and gold.

When he takes the throne of his kingdom, he is to write for himself on a scroll a copy of this law. . . . It is to be with him, and he is to read it all the days of his life so that he may learn to revere the Lord his God and follow carefully all the words of this law and these decrees and not consider himself better than his brothers and turn from the law to the right or to the left (Deuteronomy 17:14-20).

As long as Israel remained a theocracy, leadership would be viewed as merely representative of God. Moses and Joshua were God's agents, God's spokesmen. They had no inherent power of their own, whether for good or evil. But God foresaw that a king would be viewed differently. He knew that the people would see the king as having his own power and authority. He also knew that the king himself would be tempted to make the same mistake.

Also, as long as Israel remained a theocracy, power would be dispersed among the various political and religious leaders. And the power base itself would be localized with the leaders of the many tribes and clans. But once there was a king, then government and power would be nationalized, centralized, and institutionalized. The greater the power, the greater the potential for abuse of power. Hence God's instruction that the king was not to think of himself as above the law.

How is it that spiritual leaders fall into sin? They forget that they are merely God's agents and spokesmen. Like the kings of Israel who were corrupted by the power of leadership, they delude themselves into thinking they are above the law. They start thinking that the rules are made for the rest of us.

God also knew that leadership can be corrupted by exaggerated wealth. By what right was Moses or Joshua entitled to private wealth? They were just God's representatives on earth. But a king—now that would be a different story. Kings *have* to be rich. It goes with the job. It's part of the show. Of course, it is also an invitation to trouble, both for the nation and for the king. Hence God's instruction that the king was not to line his own pockets with the nation's wealth.

Spiritual leaders fall because they become victims of their own prosperity. They forget that what they have is held in trust for all the people of God. They allow themselves to be seduced by wealth, even as they preach Christ, who said of himself, "Foxes have holes and birds of the air have nests, but the Son of Man has no place to lay his head" (Luke 9:58).

If spiritual leaders have fallen because they have lined their own pockets with millions, we must ask where those millions came from. If spiritual leaders have acted as if they were above the law, we must ask who gave them that idea. I suggest that we as a church have paid the price for accepting second-best in at least two ways. In the next chapter we will take a closer look at the "Superstar Syndrome." In the following chapter we will pursue the many pitfalls of the parachurch phenomenon.

Second-best is killing the Church of England. It may also have a stranglehold on American evangelicalism for many of the same reasons. Have the spiritual superstars of our day become our "kings"? Have parachurch ministries become so powerful and affluent that our "kings" have been corrupted? Are we looking to the wrong organizations and personalities for our spiritual leadership?

The terrible price we are paying for second-best may not be worth it.

Where the Principle Hits Home

If we are beginning to see the threat of second-best to the church, we must also see the danger of second-best in our own lives. Like more recognized spiritual leaders, we too can find ourselves thinking that we are above the law. "After all, we are religious folks, aren't we? A few corners cut here and there can't be *that* bad, can it?" "After all, we don't get involved in gross immorality like the fallen televangelists, so our sins look pretty good by comparison, don't they?"

If religious elitism has not gotten us in its grasp, there is still the seductive enticement of Western affluence. Have we let rampant materialism cloud our view of the spiritual? Have we fallen prey to the self-serving prosperity preaching that saturates the airways of Christian radio and television? Have we lost the vision of sacrificial believers standing at the foot of the cross?

If in only a few short years an entire fellowship can go from denouncing makeup and jewelry to giving it exaggerated display (thereby contributing to the rise and fall of a major ministry), is it not possible for each of us to be lured into upsetting our own priorities, contributing to our own fall? Can you remember when you were poorer—and closer to God? I can. Can you remember when you had hardly anything in the world—and were happier? I can. Can you remember when you went through times of great struggle—and prayed more? I can.

When an entire church falls, surely God is waving a warning flag to the rest of us. When televangelists and other spiritual leaders fall right and left, surely bells and whistles ought to be going off. The bells are not just for spiritual leaders on the television screen, or even in the local pulpit. "Ask not for whom the bell tolls," wrote the novelist. "It tolls for thee." In looking at what happens when spiritual leaders fall, it is you and I whom we must see. We too are the fallen ones.

Looking Within

- If "the church" is more than a building, what is it? In what way are you an important part of the church?
- Is your church vibrant and alive, or is it in decline? What factors have brought it to the point where you find it?
- Are there any ways in which you have contributed to the fall of a spiritual leader or the church? If so, is there anything you can do about it now?
- Is your own relationship with God vibrant and alive, or is it in decline? What factors—good or bad—have contributed to the level of spirituality you see in yourself?
- What is there in your life that honesty would force you to recognize as second-best before the Lord?

7

The Superstar Syndrome

Elevating the Few

Peter Thompson (not his real name), deacon in a prominent Baptist church in a major Southern city, recently pleaded guilty to two counts of embezzlement and was given five years probation upon the condition that he pay back the $10,000 he had stolen from church funds while he acted as church treasurer. The money had been used to buy a car for a woman with whom Thompson was having an affair, a woman he later married after divorcing his wife. Following a church disciplinary proceeding, the church disfellowshipped Thompson and read his dismissal letter to the congregation. The criminal action never made the newspapers.

In March 1987, Jim Bakker, cohost of the popular PTL television show, resigned as Chairman of the Board of the PTL Ministries, amid disclosures of sexual misconduct and the use of $265,000 of ministry money to pay off Jessica Hahn, the former church secretary who had been involved in the incident. Bakker's name dominated national media attention for months afterward.

What was the difference between the sins of Peter Thompson and Jim Bakker? What was the difference in impact on the Christian community?

John Miller (again, not his real name), a Presbyterian minister in a small Iowa town, was dismissed from his position after it was learned that he had visited a sleazy massage parlor near Chicago's O'Hare Airport while attending a church conference. Members of Miller's congregation were shocked and disappointed, but few people outside his own church and family ever knew about the incident. The local paper carried a brief article on the change of ministers at the church, but never referred to the reason for Miller's leaving.

Jimmy Swaggart, a television evangelist whose programs are broadcast around the world, was relieved of his duties as copastor of the Family Worship Center in Baton Rouge, Louisiana, and ordered not to preach for a one-year period after it was learned that he had engaged a prostitute for purposes of lewd conduct. The incident became front-page headlines across the world, causing many people to grieve and others to scorn what they called his "Oscar-winning confession."

What was the difference between the sins of John Miller and Jimmy Swaggart? What was the difference in impact on the Christian community?

In each case the sins were equally disgraceful. But only in the cases of Bakker and Swaggart did their high profiles cause widespread disgrace to the whole Christian community. The obscure falls of Thompson and Miller (whose fictionalized names and cases represent any number of real spiritual leaders caught up in those situations) caused but a ripple. Should the Bakker-Swaggart kind of vulnerability to exposure ever have been possible? Would it have been possible in the New Testament church?

Presumably the apostle Paul's inner struggle with temptation could have been a matter of catastrophic disgrace for the whole church if he had yielded to any kind of immorality. Fortunately, despite whatever spiritual struggles he might have encountered, Paul remained a steadfast pillar of righteousness throughout his life.

Although the original 12 apostles dishonored themselves through excessive pride and political bickering— and, with Judas, even through betrayal—fortunately, the remaining 11 led the young church with impeccable character and moral courage after being filled with the Holy Spirit. (Peter's hypocrisy, noted in Galatians chapter 2, being the possible exception.) But it was never intended that the apostles' unique positions would be continued throughout ensuing generations—and undoubtedly with good reason.

Departure from the Pattern

Who then took the apostles' place in the first century church? Evangelists? Elders? Deacons? Actually, no one ever replaced the apostles; rather, local spiritual leaders were appointed even before the apostles' deaths, in order to ensure continuity of leadership throughout the church. Two evangelists, Titus and Timothy, were specifically commissioned to appoint local leaders in the young churches with whom they had been working. As Paul wrote to Titus, "The reason I left you in Crete was that you might straighten out what was left unfinished and appoint elders in every town, as I directed you" (Titus 1:5).

Paul laid down the qualifications for both elders and deacons, which we find in his letters to Titus and Timothy. The elders, or spiritual overseers, were to be local leaders, with responsibility for shepherding the members within their respective congregations. In his first letter Peter gives us a flavor of their duties and responsibilities:

> To the elders among you, I appeal as a fellow elder, a witness of Christ's sufferings and one who also will share in the glory to be revealed: Be shepherds of God's flock that is under your care, serving as overseers—not because you must, but because you are willing, as God wants you to be; not greedy for money, but eager to serve; not lording it over those entrusted to you, but being examples to the flock.

> And when the Chief Shepherd appears, you
> will receive the crown of glory that will never
> fade away (1 Peter 5:1-4).

These men—referred to alternately as elders, over-seers, bishops, presbyters, shepherds, or pastors—were to direct the affairs of the church, not simply for the purpose of building church buildings or providing other material needs of the congregation, but primarily for the spiritual building up of the body of Christ (Ephesians 4:12).

Often, if not usually, the elders themselves performed the teaching function of the person we would recognize today as the local preacher. Many of them were supported financially in order to carry out the work of teaching on a full-time basis. Paul had told Timothy, for example, "The elders who direct the affairs of the church well are worthy of double honor, especially those whose work is preaching and teaching" (1 Timothy 5:17).

Hence our tendency today to think of elders (who oversee) and pastors (who preach) as being two different roles is probably an unwarranted and unwise separation. If we are to have "pastors" in the church, for example, have we stopped to consider whether they meet the New Testament qualifications for pastors-slash-elders? In the first century, pastors and elders were one and the same.

I recognize that many people today see no reason to follow the first-century pattern, believing that those forms were applicable to that day and culture but that we are free to evolve our own systems. However, if the patterns of the first century were set down by inspired spokesmen, as most of us believe, then certainly they are *first*-best, not second-best. We have no such guarantee when it comes to our own inventions.

Unfortunately, over the next several centuries the localization of spiritual leaders gradually expanded into an interwoven hierarchy. Local elders, wishing to have influence outside their own congregations, began to assume to themselves the leadership of larger and larger groups of congregations. Eventually local bishops were subsumed by head bishops, and then archbishops, leading ultimately to the establishment of the office of Pope. The process was very much more complex than that, of course. Nevertheless, the first-century pattern of exclusive local leadership was virtually abandoned.

Unfortunately, this departure led to a variety of institutionalized abuses, not unlike those anticipated by God himself when he reluctantly permitted Israel to have a king. How much more could one be "above the law," for example, than when he claims infallibility while speaking "ex cathedra"! Hierarchy breeds heresy. It elevates one spiritual leader over others such that *his* word becomes *the* word. By contrast, congregational independence, with all spiritual leadership on the same level, promotes free inquiry and unfettered biblical practice.

When the local elders' sphere of influence is limited to the flock of God over which they are spiritual shepherds, there is congregational autonomy. No one tells them how to read the Scriptures, and they dictate to no one else what doctrine ought to be believed. Like the noble Bereans (Acts 17), each independent congregation of the Lord's people can search the Scriptures for themselves to determine God's will for their work and worship. No council, assembly, synod, conference, or other hierarchical board can be in a position to potentially perpetuate doctrinal error by nationwide or worldwide mandate.

There is a certain irony in the fact that, while we evangelicals would reject as unbiblical the ecclesiastical hierarchy of Catholicism and even Anglicanism, we feel comfortable having a handful of superleaders, sometimes from radically different theological persuasions, who presume to speak on behalf of the entire evangelical Christian community. These are America's "super-evangelists," whose holy war over PTL, for example, saw intrigues of power and control worthy of the darkest annals of medieval church history.

In permitting superstar leadership have we accepted second-best, only to inherit the very problems we criticize in other people?

Evangelists or Super-evangelists?

Perhaps we have misunderstood the role of the evangelist. Perhaps we have allowed the evangelist to become an independent entity lacking personal accountability. When Titus and Timothy went around appointing local spiritual leaders, did they set a precedent for evangelists to be superleaders? Or was their mission unique to the needs of the infant, first-century church?

We certainly don't get the idea from the Scriptures that the elders were simply a lay board of directors, hiring out and approving the work of the church to be done by a more professional clergy. If there was any clergy at all—which, biblically speaking, is highly questionable—then the elders *were* the clergy. They did more than build sheep pens and hire independent contractors to work with the sheep. *They* were the shepherds; *they* fed the sheep.

Instead of complaining about "battered pastors" playing like a one-man band the roles of preacher, teacher, administrator, counselor, visitor, political activist, social director, and community relations director, perhaps it is time that we rethought how far we have come from the New Testament pattern of spiritual leadership. How we have funneled what was meant to be diversified leadership into a single position within the church. How we have downplayed the spiritual responsibilities of the local overseers.

If New Testament pastor-elders played a more central role in feeding the local sheep, what then was the role of the evangelist? Paul gave Timothy the charge: "Preach the Word; be prepared in season and out of season; correct, rebuke and encourage—with great patience and careful instruction" (2 Timothy 4:2). And again, "the things you have heard me say in the presence of many witnesses entrust to reliable men who will also be qualified to teach others" (2 Timothy 2:2).

Whether Titus and Timothy, or even Philip the evangelist, were intended to be typical of future evangelists is unclear. It appears that their responsibilities extended to more than one congregation, much like the circuit-riding preachers on the American frontier. The breadth of their ministry may or may not have been a unique phenomenon of the infant church, but in any case it did not compete with the oversight and spiritual feeding to be done by the local presbytery.

What we *do* know about evangelists is that, first and foremost, they were proclaimers of the gospel. They were not showmen, entertainers, or superstar media personalities. Their job was to convict sinners; to bring lost souls to Christ; to bring them into local fellowships where godly spiritual shepherds could feed them, up close and personal. They didn't have their own fan clubs, made up of unknown faces, sitting in unknown homes, tuning in at unknown times.

It was Jesus who stressed the importance of the shepherd knowing his own sheep. In what way, other than through a local congregation, can the shepherds know the sheep and their needs in order to meet those needs? That is a work which, even if they wanted to, televangelists simply cannot do.

Hoisted on Our Own Petards

National and international proclamation of the gospel through the media of radio and television ought to be a blessing to the cause of Christ, and in many cases it has been. But it has also been a springboard for a brand of spiritual leadership which threatens that very cause.

Given the nature of even the secular media, the problem is built in. Television, even more than radio, demands glitz and pizzazz. There must be drama and melodrama, action and interaction. Gone are the days of the dry newsreader. No respectable network today would dare have its newscast presented by anyone lacking an affable, upbeat, and winning personality. As well as *presenting* the news, the news anchors themselves *are* the news. Ratings, which dictate the network's financial success or failure, depend upon getting just the right face in front of the camera. Program content runs a distant second.

Sadly, the same is true of Christian television. To keep vastly expensive broadcasts, stations, and networks afloat, the money has to keep coming in, program after program, day in and day out. I don't envy those who shoulder the budgetary burdens. But whether we are victims of what we've come to expect in the secular media or whether it is in our nature to love a show, the name of the game is still glitz, pizzazz, and personality. If you've got glamorous, star-quality hosts or fire-breathing, miracle-working evangelists, you survive. If not, you close the doors and go home.

Few Christian television programs succeed when all that is shown is a godly man of the Word sitting before the open Book, quietly gleaning its rich teaching and helping the listener to apply the Word to his or her life. You've got to turn up the volume and quicken the pace. In fact, what you've got to do above all else is to entertain. And "entertainment" is not all pop gospel singers, talk-show interviews, and audience participation. Entertainment can also be carefully orchestrated worship services, dramatic healing sessions, and teary-eyed preaching.

Without anyone subversively plotting it, there is a most interesting natural progression in Christian television, leading to some scary conclusions. First is the inevitable success of the more-spectacular programs over the less-spectacular programs. Second is the fact that spectacular programs tend to be more consistent with Pentecostal fellowships than with any other fellowships. Third, what results is a virtual monopoly of the airwaves by one brand of Christianity. Fourth, when the secular viewer turns on religious television, it is that particular perspective he is exposed to, and which he thinks represents all Christianity. And fifth, it is Christianity in general which he blames when the individuals featured on Christian television fall into public disgrace.

Of course, he doesn't stop to think that the actions of the superstar may be as repulsive to members of the evangelist's own fellowship as to himself. Nor does he consider how many righteous believers would never have sent in a dollar of support if they had had even the faintest notion what was going on behind the scenes. Yet in his mind—and in the minds of the millions of skeptical viewers just like him—*all* of us in the Christian community have fallen into disrepute.

Remember, it's the big picture we are concerned about here. In the big picture, superstar evangelists become synonymous with Christian television, and Christian television becomes synonymous with Christianity. In the eyes of the world, when the superstars fall, so falls Christianity. Worse still, when Christianity falls in the eyes of the world, so may their regard for the Person of Jesus Christ.

Can we possibly imagine how many souls will reject their own salvation through Jesus Christ simply because of the fall of a few scandalized ministries? Who are the unknown viewers out there who hold Christ in contempt because of fallen televangelists?

And who are the people around the rest of us every day who reject faith in Christ because of the image that *we ourselves* present of Christianity? Whether superstars or simple folk, we are the key that unlocks the door of salvation to those who look to us for examples of spiritual strength and godliness.

Second-Best Begs Trouble

The very prospect of all of this is enough to make one appreciate the wisdom of New Testament leadership—local and dispersed—in which the fall of any one spiritual leader will have minimal effect on the church. In military terms, you wouldn't think of having just a handful of supercarriers as your entire navy. If they get shot out of the water, you are left defenseless. Rather, you would have *many* ships well-dispersed among the enemy. Few targets become big targets; big targets invite defeat.

So where have we gone wrong? Was it in the use of television? Of course not. Television for us is what the mountain was for Jesus—the best place to reach the most people. Was it in the presentation of the power of Christianity and the joyous praise of our God? No. Jesus himself got the attention of the crowds when he performed miracles in their presence. Was it in preaching hellfire and judgment? Again, no. The more John the Baptist preached repentance, the more he packed them in.

Where we have gone wrong is in putting men before the message; presentation before proclamation; evangelists before evangelism.

In insisting on having "the very best" in our pulpits and in front of television cameras, we've too often settled for second-best. Few of God's men through the centuries would have been the natural choice for spiritual leaders. They certainly would not lend much grace to our pulpits today. And hardly any would have fit the job description for a television ministry, even if they had had television. Like Moses, many of God's chosen leaders were shy and reticent, unsure of their own abilities. Like Jonah, many of them didn't even want the job of being "God's man."

It is a familiar passage, but it bears re-reading. In it, Paul all but tells us that even he would not be on our present-day short list of big-name superstars:

> When I came to you, brothers, I did not come with eloquence or superior wisdom as I proclaimed to you the testimony about God. For I resolved to know nothing while I was with you except Jesus Christ and him crucified. I came to you in weakness and fear, and with much trembling. My message and my preaching were not with wise and persuasive words, but with a demonstration of the Spirit's power, so that your faith might not rest on men's wisdom, but on God's power (1 Corinthians 2:1-5).

How long would a weak preacher like that last on Christian television? Undoubtedly, the camera close-ups would pick up the fear and trembling.

Where we have gone wrong is in allowing Christian television to follow the natural course of secular television—to elevate to stardom men and women who can't possibly bear the burden of being spiritual superstars.

Why do Christian media superstars fall? Because we rocket them into outer space, and then wonder why they never come back down to earth. We make them shooting stars, and then act surprised when they fizzle out. We make them matinee idols, and then can't understand why they idolize themselves.

Men or Gods?

Of course, it doesn't take television for the ego trip to

get out of control. That problem has been around since at least the time of Paul and Barnabas. While in the city of Lystra on his first missionary journey, Paul healed a man who had been crippled and lame from birth. Nothing unusual about that for Paul. What *was* unusual was the reaction of the crowd:

> When the crowd saw what Paul had done, they shouted in the Lycaonian language, "The gods have come down to us in human form!" Barnabas they called Zeus, and Paul they called Hermes because he was the chief speaker. The priest of Zeus, whose temple was just outside the city, brought bulls and wreaths to the city gates because he and the crowd wanted to offer sacrifices to them (Acts 14:11-13).

Whether in the dusty streets of an ancient Turkish town or in the civic auditorium rented by the traveling faith healer or on camera before millions of eager on-lookers—when men of faith are believed to have performed miracles, they take on a kind of godlike quality. "Who can do these things, except God be with him?" asks the believer in the crowd.

The miracle-worker is superhuman. He has a power that the rest of us don't have. You can praise a preacher of the Word, but a miracle-worker is something else again. A miracle-worker is worthy of adulation; he stands right up there next to God himself. Or so we sometimes think.

Paul and Barnabas might well have warmed to the occasion and accepted the crowd-worship being offered to them. Lesser men would have done so. I dare say few of us would not have felt at least a twinge of schizo-phrenia at the moment. If the smallest compliment makes us feel good all over, imagine the temptation when a crowd of admirers wants to worship you! For-tunately, in this case that temptation was overcome:

> But when the apostles Barnabas and Paul
> heard of this, they tore their clothes and rushed
> into the crowd, shouting: "Men, why are you
> doing this? We too are only men, human like
> you. We are bringing you good news, telling you
> to turn from these worthless things to the living
> God, who made heaven and earth and sea and
> everything in them." . . . Even with these words,
> they had difficulty keeping the crowd from sac-
> rificing to them (Acts 14:14,15,18).

The exercise of spiritual gifts has never been without
risks. He who would assume the mantle of a miracle-
worker walks on the slippery precipice of pride. And all
it takes for a predictable fall is for awestruck crowds to
provide the slightest nudge in that direction.

If anyone had a right to accept worship, it was Jesus
himself. Yet he knew, better than we do, that adulation
for spiritual leaders—especially "miracle-workers"—
comes all too easily, for a host of wrong reasons. He also
must have felt the temptation to "warm to the occasion."
But he fled that temptation.

> After the people saw the miraculous sign
> that Jesus did, they began to say, "Surely this is
> the Prophet who is to come into the world."
> Jesus, knowing that they intended to come and
> make him king by force, withdrew again into
> the hills by himself (John 6:14,15).

Jesus would have been justified to accept the kingship
the people wanted to bestow on him, for he *was* their
King. But they didn't understand the spiritual nature of
his kingdom. He had not come to heal bodies, but broken relationships. He had not come to feed empty
stomachs, but empty lives. He had not come to give sight

to the blind, but insight to the lost. If he ever sensed that his miracles were taking the spotlight from his message, he took another course.

Sometimes today one gets the idea that it's the miracles that are most important. Or, God forbid, the miracle-worker himself.

Jesus set a good example for all spiritual leaders: He simply made himself unavailable to those who would elevate him for wrong reasons. And so should we. If we ever look out into the audience and catch a glimpse of eyes sprinkled with a bit of awe, it's time we remembered what Paul said to the crowd in Lystra: "We too are only men, human like you."

Is it possible that some have succumbed to sin because the miracle of humility has eluded the "miracle-worker" to whom the crowd has offered its adulation?

False Heroes

A few years ago I was in the Midwest, familiarizing people with *The Narrated Bible*, which had just been published. At one stop a well-intentioned brother in my fellowship took me aside and complimented me on the work I had done in producing it. He then took me aback when he said, "LaGard, we need to position you in the church so that you can get as much exposure as possible." I was flattered, of course, but I could tell he didn't know me as well as I knew me. When I protested, he said something further that sounded right, but hit me wrong. "The church needs a hero," he tried to assure me.

It sounded right, because all my life I have admired the heroes of the Bible. To walk down the Hall of Faith in Hebrews chapter 11—to read about Abel, Enoch, Noah, Abraham, Joseph, Moses, and the other spiritual giants through the centuries—just about takes one's breath away. So, "Maybe he's right," I thought. "Maybe we do need modern-day heroes in the church"—though certainly I was not prepared to be one of them. I wasn't hero material.

Later I thought about the difference between the heroes of old and the heroes of today. What struck me was that the heroes in the Bible were rarely recognized as heroes in their own time. To the contrary, their contemporaries often thought they were quite mad, or even found them threatening. And certainly they did not receive a hero's welcome wherever they went. In fact, the writer of Hebrews paints a quite different picture:

> [They] were tortured and refused to be released, so that they might gain a better resurrection. Some faced jeers and flogging, while still others were chained and put in prison. They were stoned; they were sawed in two; they were put to death by the sword. They went about in sheepskins and goatskins, destitute, persecuted and mistreated.... They wandered in deserts and mountains, and in caves and holes in the ground (Hebrews 11:35-38).

Few of these heroes of faith would have been comfortable on the superstar stage of today's Christian ministry. The floodlights of the television studio would blind the eyes of those who had fled to caves to escape godless enemies seeking to kill them. The cheers of an appreciative audience would likely confuse them; all they knew were hostile jeers. And as for tailored suits, makeup, and Rolex watches, they would never have believed it. Too many of them had managed to survive in tattered goatskins while pleading with a sinful world to turn back to God.

I purposely omitted from the passage above one of the most moving epitaphs of all time. It deserves a solo appearance. It should be read with reverence and awe, for it is holy ground on which we walk. Bestowing uncommon honor, the inspired writer wrote simply, "The world was not worthy of them."

How many of our modern-day heroes of success-oriented ministries would have made the grade? Of whom today could it be said, "The world was not worthy of them"?

Yes, the church *does* need a hero, a divine hero. But none of us is qualified for the job. We are privileged to know Jesus but forget who he is, when by contrast the heroes of faith lived sacrificial lives in mere anticipation without ever seeing him. "Therefore, since we are surrounded by such a great cloud of witnesses . . . let us fix our eyes on Jesus, the author and perfecter of our faith, who for the joy set before him endured the cross, scorning its shame, and sat down at the right hand of the throne of God" (Hebrews 12:1,2).

Jesus Christ should be hero enough for any of us. It is he alone upon whom we must fix our sights. Although I've never particularly appreciated the reference to "Jesus Christ, Superstar," he must be our only choice if we are forced to choose. No other superstar will do.

Why do spiritual leaders fall? Because we insist on making them heroes when that position has already been filled.

Looking Within

- Who is the most influential spiritual leader in your life—a televangelist, a local preacher, or an elder in your congregation? Does he fit the biblical pattern of spiritual leadership?
- If the one to whom you look for spiritual leadership were himself to fall, how would your relationship with God be different? Would your relationship with the church be affected?

- In what ways has the church courted danger by elevating to prominence a few of its leaders?
- What are the special dangers facing those who are featured prominently on Christian radio and television?
- How do your heroes of faith compare with the heroes of faith in the Bible? How do they compare with Christ?

8

Problems in the Parachurch

Ministries as Church Substitutes

Terminal One at Los Angeles International Airport was more crowded than usual, and USAir flight 26 to Pittsburgh looked full. I was discouraged because I had hoped to pull out my computer during the flight and get some work done. My boarding pass indicated a middle seat, giving me little hope of having sufficient elbow room in which to work. I decided to play the odds that there might be a window or aisle seat left over, so I waited to be the very last in line.

As I entered the plane, my hopes were rewarded. Amazingly, in an otherwise completely full plane, both the window seat and the middle seat next to it in the second row were vacant. I clamored clumsily past the passenger in the aisle seat, and had just sat down in the window seat, when another passenger appeared from out of nowhere and gave me that "hey-buster-you're-in-my-seat" look.

As I slid to the middle seat, it occurred to me that both my briefcase and my computer would not fit under the seat in front of me. With great embarrassment I indicated to the big guy on the aisle that I needed to get out again. He must have thought I was a real idiot as I shoved my briefcase into the overhead rack, and then my sport coat for good measure.

Then, out of the corner of my eye, I suddenly recognized the huge hulk of a man waiting patiently for me to sort myself out: It was comedian Jay Leno. I had seen him just the night before guest-hosting for Johnny Carson. "Sorry to cause such grief for someone whose work I admire so much," I turned and said. He smiled and laughed that staccato laugh which has become his trademark. Yep, it was definitely Jay Leno, exaggerated chin and all.

As we finally got buckled into our seats, we heard the Captain give us the bad news that it would be another ten minutes before we would be cleared to leave the ramp. Leno was grousing about the delay, the soaring temperature in the cabin, and, most of all, the fact that "Row 2" was not in First Class. It was his first experience with USAir, and he had assumed he would be flying First Class, as always. Leno wasn't just being snooty; he simply didn't fit into the seat!

Once in the air, we made small talk about his work and where he was going. I couldn't wait to get Leno's reaction to my destination that day. As often as I had heard him poke fun at the PTL scandal, I thought he might be intrigued to learn that, at that very moment, I was on my way to make an appearance on the "PTL Show." Sure enough, when he dropped the question into my lap "Where 'ya headed?" my response caused him to literally draw back his big frame and look me directly in the eye. "*Why*, for goodness sake?" he asked, disbelieving. His face maintained that look of incredulity mixed with curiosity as I told him I was going to be interviewed about two of my books.

It gave me the opening I had hoped for. I told him a friend of mine had commented to me that he thought Leno was unusually moral for a comedian. At first a big smile crossed his face, and then he immediately became somber. For a long time he seemed to be turning that thought around in his mind. "What are you, religiously?" I ventured. "Well, I dunno," he drawled thoughtfully. "I guess I'm ... Protestant," he said after a long pause.

"Most people would think I'm a Christian. I don't drink, or smoke, or fool around on my wife." Then, shifting his eyes as if to see whether anyone were looking, he said in kind of a secretive hush, "I've never even smoked a joint."

The conversation led to my book, *Out on a Broken Limb*, and to Shirley MacLaine's belief in reincarnation. Leno believed in God, but wasn't sure about an afterlife. "I don't really think about it," he mused. But I guessed he was too bright and contemplative not to have given the subject at least a once-over at some point in his life. And I did sense that his values were unusually straight, despite his uncertainty about God and about life after death.

As we prepared for landing, one of the men in the row in front of us passed back a newspaper for Leno to sign, which he did with a smile. Of course I got his autograph too—but only for a friend of mine. No, really! Then I signed and gave him a copy of *Out on a Broken Limb*, telling him he should carry it with him just in case he ever had trouble sleeping. "One chapter and it'll put you right out," I assured him with a smile. I secretly hoped, of course, that he might read it in earnest and come to know Christ in his life. I don't know whether he ever read it. Two nights later, on "The Tonight Show," Shirley MacLaine was the target of several Jay Leno punch lines.

It later occurred to me that I had sat next to a guy who regularly appears before more people than anyone on the "PTL Show." And there he was, night after night on "The Tonight Show," joining with America in a good laugh at PTL's expense. "Would it ever be possible," I wondered, "to reach a guy like Jay Leno with the message of the gospel, and, perhaps through him, millions of other skeptics?" Scandal in the Christian community was having a devastating impact. Was it because, in our efforts to serve God, we had settled for second-best?

Conversion of a Skeptic—Almost

After a change of planes in Pittsburgh, I finally landed at the Charlotte, North Carolina, airport. There I was met by PTL's driver, Allen Hopkins, a clean-cut, affable young man who directed me to a shiny (unstretched) limo. I sat in the front seat with my host, and we headed for the PTL complex in Fort Mill, just across the state line into South Carolina. It was November 18. As we turned onto the grounds of the complex, the entry and main road were aglow with hundreds of both real and artificial trees lighted for the Christmas season. The official opening of Heritage USA's "Christmas City" was to be that weekend. "Glitz and pizzazz, right at the front entrance," I thought to myself.

As we parked under the portico of the enormous Heritage Grand Hotel and walked through the front entrance, I was surprised at the immense atrium-style lobby, complete with swimming pool and glass-bubbled elevators. No shoestring operation this!

My room on the second floor was actually two standard rooms joined as a suite. As I entered, a sign on the door displayed the name of a donor who, I thought I recalled from PTL literature, was privileged to use the suite for a week or so each year. Inside I found rich carpeting, lovely cherry-wood furniture, and two televisions—one in the lounge and one in the bedroom.

Bay windows in each room looked out onto the Main Street of Heritage Village. The "street" is actually a mall containing a score or more shops and eateries. The vaulted blue ceiling assures perpetual blue skies regardless of the weather outside or the time of day. It took heavy curtains to shield out the artificial daylight on the artificial street in this artificial turn-of-the-century piece of Americana.

After dinner I strolled around the hotel lobby and along Main Street. Not surprisingly, the bookshop captured my attention first. I was impressed with its size and selection of Christian books and music, and even more pleased to see that copies of my books were on the shelf. (I resisted the classical author's temptation to turn my books face-out to the customers' view!)

Perhaps it was seeing my books in the middle of Heritage USA that began to turn the tide in my attitude. I had come, frankly, as a skeptic. But, I'm sure that what really turned the tide for me was the people. Everyone I met treated me like "home folk." It was comfortable. It was family. More than once I caught myself comparing the hotel and its recreation facilities to other hotels and amusement centers. It took little effort to appreciate the superiority of a place filled with people of faith. I felt a kinship with the commonness that milled in a leisurely way about the artificially opulent facade. The guests were just ordinary people sharing simple family pleasures. There was no show with them. No pizzazz.

Back in Malibu, people might scorn the glitzy PTL image, but I wondered about that. There were no Polo sport shirts or Armani suits on these people. The only Dior tie I noticed in the whole place was the one hanging around my own neck. The parking lot wasn't filled with the BMW and Mercedes Benz status symbols of Southern California. It was pretty much a Ford and Chevy crowd. If the charge were Embarrassingly Ostentatious, the visitors, at least, were Not Guilty.

Back in my room I flipped on the television in the lounge. Other channels were available, but the TV happened to be tuned to PTL's own programming—this night a fund-raising marathon. The timing couldn't have been worse. I had just gained a new appreciation for PTL, and now all I saw were hyper personalities working the television crowd for contributions. It smacked of commercial hucksterism and showbiz gimmickry. I turned it off and wondered what in the world I was doing there. *Promoting books* is what I was doing there! Christian books! Was I too a huckster?

The next morning I was taken to the television studio. The "green room," as all TV-guest waiting rooms are called, was the plushest I had ever seen, even at major network affiliates. The faces I had seen on the marathon the previous night began filling the room. One by one they went into makeup. At last it was my turn. On went the apron, and here came the cover cream. What they saved on my bearded face was made up for amply on my bald head.

Backstage I kept wondering what I was doing there. My friends, who know that I am far from being a charismatic, had enjoyed a great laugh when they learned I was to be on PTL. If politics makes strange bedfellows, religion even more so. But I felt I had a message to share, not just books to promote.

The message? That one of the reasons we get into trouble, like PTL had gotten into trouble, is that we let emotion (itself a good thing) hold sway over reason (also a good thing). Instead of being people of the Word, we become people of *people*.

In fact, the problem ends up being circular. Our biblical illiteracy tends to make us rely on evangelists—superevangelists or otherwise. And our reliance on evangelists—particularly those who put themselves before the Word—leads, in turn, to biblical illiteracy. If I could get that message across, then I could promote *The Narrated Bible* in good conscience as a helpful way to get us all back into the written Word.

I was greatly relieved to learn that I would be interviewed by Ron Aldridge and Brenda Davis. I found them to be bright, conscientious, and sincere young people. Sitting between them, I was back with comfortable "common folk" again, just like the people in the audience whom I had seen the night before on Main Street. Here I was on the set of the "PTL Show," and I actually felt at home!

I'm not sure how well I got my message across in the few minutes we had, but I tried to say what was on my heart. I left the PTL complex with mixed feelings. Although I had gained a new appreciation for the regular folks whose money goes to support the cause, and had met two young people who are the kind of people it will take to turn PTL around, I still sensed that something was not right.

There was still too much time spent begging for money in a place where *faith* is given so much prominence. Still too much orchestrated excitement and too little quiet talk about our relationship with God. Still too much "entertainment" in an hour devoted to spiritual concern. Still too many frenetic personalities in the forefront. Still too much glitz and pizzazz.

The Nature of the Beast

Months later now, as I reflect on PTL—and, yes, CBN, TBN, The Jimmy Swaggart Ministries, The Hour of Power, The Oral Roberts Evangelistic Association, and all the other ministries—I see problems painted on a much broader canvass. The recently publicized disasters should have come as no surprise. The problems associated with so many ministries today are inevitable, unavoidable, and inescapable.

It's the nature of the beast, which in this case is the whole parachurch phenomenon. "Parachurch" includes the hundreds of independent ministries throughout the country—often involved in radio and television programs—and other church-related, yet church-distinct, Christian organizations. The parachurch phenomenon is a hungry beast which never stops being hungry. Over and over again it demands to be fed. It growls and threatens disaster if you ignore it. And even when you feed it, it can turn on you. It devours its superstar trainers and bites the millions of hands that feed it.

As Van Nuys Baptist's Jess Moody remarked recently in somewhat of a different context, "Preachers are creatures who create monsters who eat them."

Why should that be, if indeed parachurch organizations are Christian endeavors? If God's hand is in them, why is there so much pain and suffering? Why such disgrace? It's too easy to dismiss recent scandals as the problem of human fallibility, common to every earthly effort on behalf of Christ, including his church. With parachurch organizations—whether media organizations or other evangelism outreach programs—the stakes are higher. The falls, when they occur, are greater. The anguish for the whole Christian community is intensified and multiplied.

The Parachurch: Best or Second-Best?

I'm convinced we are running afoul of the age-old principle we have been seeing over and over. In parachurch organizations we are dealing with second-best, which—as always—is bound to have problems. The very word "parachurch" ought to be a clue. "Parachurch" is *not* the church. "Parachurch" is something *other* than the church, something *beyond* the church.

It is *the church* Christ died for, not the "parachurch." It is *the church* that is the bride of Christ, not the "parachurch." It is *the church* to which the saved are added, not the "parachurch." It is through *the church* that the manifold wisdom of God is made known, not through the "parachurch."

It is not simply a matter of semantics, and it's more than playing word games. There are essential and functional differences between the church and parachurch organizations. For the church, there is a scriptural pattern of work and worship. For parachurch organizations, human creativity is the limit of all possibilities. For the church, financial solvency follows from biblical principles of cheerful giving. For parachurch organizations, there is too much evidence of giving done from guilt, emotional coercion, and gimmickry. For the church, financial accountability is the responsibility of grass-roots spiritual oversight. For parachurch organizations, financial accountability may be the sole responsibility of next of kin.

If necessary, the church could survive forever without even the widow's mite. Few parachurch organizations, if any, could last more than a day without substantial donations. The church could exist for centuries without a single superleader. Few parachurch organizations could.

"Parachurch" means *like* the church, but not the same. Similar but different. And, just as with dangerous frauds the greater the similarity, the greater the deception.

In My Own Backyard

Just in case you think I am rattling someone else's cage unnecessarily, let me assure you that problems with parachurch organizations are as close to home as my own backyard. Indeed, as close as my own paycheck. Christian colleges and universities are no less para-church organizations than television ministries. They may be "church-related," but they are not the church. Like most television ministries, they are founded by Christians, funded by Christians, run by Christians, and attended by Christians, but they are not the church.

In most cases Christian colleges operate independently from churches, under boards of directors who may or may not be associated with a given church. More often than not, funds for operation of the institution come from private donations, and must be maintained in large amounts to balance precarious budgets.

Certainly there is wisdom in the basic idea of separating from the church such parachurch organizations as television ministries and Christian colleges. Because they often perform functions the church was never intended to perform, any closer ties would threaten the church's primary mission.

A delicate balance must be struck. All one has to do is look at the secularization of Harvard, Yale, Columbia, and scores of other academic institutions which long ago cut ties with their founding churches, in order to appreciate what can happen when parachurch organizations stray too far from the body of Christ. On the other hand, it doesn't take much reflection to appreciate the disasters which occur when the church gets tangled up in the business of secular education or independently run evangelistic organizations.

The fact that parachurch organizations can sometimes do what the church cannot may justify in some instances our walking that precarious line for the good that can be accomplished. But we walk that line at the risk of paying parachurch prices.

In Christian colleges, for example, we have had to pay the price of parachurch glitz and pizzazz. Gone are the days when Christian colleges could raise sufficient donations from a handshake and a prayer. Any Christian college wanting to keep its doors open today must cater to the wealthy, through all sorts of fund-raising strategies. Although it rarely approaches the gimmickry of hard-sell Christian television, it nevertheless usually requires the outlay of vast sums of money.

To get money these days, you have to spend money. That's nothing new to any private college administrator anywhere. But in the case of Christian colleges, the world looks askance at the efforts of what they perceive to be affluent Christian institutions preparing young people to go out into a not-so-affluent world to serve their fellowman.

As another part of their fund-raising strategy, it is not uncommon for Christian colleges and universities to seek out presidents and other top administrators with charismatic personalities who can impress potential donors with the aims and goals of the institution. Nor is it uncommon for university administrators to be men who have achieved recognition as outstanding spiritual leaders within their given fellowships. Over the years, more than a few of these have had falls from grace not unlike notable televangelists. And the negative impact, both within the Christian community and beyond, has brought predictable disgrace, not only to the Christian colleges, but to the church as well.

Of course, the potential for disgrace runs the entire gamut, from administration to faculty to staff. And this is particularly true when the ties are close between the university and the church. On our campus, for example, the ties with the church are far less structured than with many other church-related colleges. Even so, our students—particularly our non-Christian students—are highly sensitive to what ties do exist.

They point to the fact that many of the elders and deacons of the church which meets on campus are also members of the university's faculty and administration. Because the university is like a small community, this overlapping of roles should not be surprising. Nonetheless, in the minds of many students the university is the church and the church is the university. From their critical perspective, as the university goes, so goes the church. If the university operates on a high moral level, then the reputation of the church is enhanced. But when we who are part of the administration, faculty, or staff fall spiritually, we torpedo the efforts of the church to be an influence for good among those we serve.

One further risk we might mention is common to virtually all parachurch organizations, but perhaps more easily seen in Christian colleges. It is the risk that the tail will wag the dog. By virtue of sheer visibility, fiscal superiority, and scope of influence, Christian colleges can actually dwarf the churches with which they are tied. It can happen when highly respected university leaders are perceived to speak on behalf of the church itself; when what is taught at Christian colleges influences the thinking of the church in the next generation; and when Christian college campuses become the "Mars Hills" of doctrinal discussion within a fellowship.

Apply those same risks to parachurch television ministries and you will get similar results. The risks of parachurch organizations, in whatever form they might exist, always seem the same. When we *look* in every respect like the church but are in fact *different* from the church, we are bound to confuse a lot of people, often even ourselves.

So unique is each parachurch organization that no one set of guidelines would be appropriate for all. However, recent scandals would suggest the wisdom of structuring ministries in such a way that no one person is constantly in the limelight. Even in the area of fundraising, a team approach is now serving many Christian colleges even better than the old style super-fund-raiser. Not only would a team approach to ministry act as damage control should a spiritual leader fall, but it would also prevent the kind of personality worship that tends to take place among people searching for superstars.

If it is argued that such a plan, even if more biblical, is practicably unworkable, then that conclusion ought to cause us to reconsider the advisability of having such a ministry in the first place. If it really won't work any other way, perhaps it is not *meant* to work. Are we willing to let go of what we hold dear and do it God's way?

Do too many people have a vested interest in the continuation of ministries which are already in place? If so, is it possible that recent scandals are God's way of once again throwing the money-changers out of the temple? Surely we can no longer afford to assume that

God has no insight into human nature and how we best function, or that he is ill-informed about how his work can best be accomplished. There is one thing we can count on: If our efforts are of God, they will succeed; if they are not of God, they are bound to fail!

Close Only Counts in Horseshoes

This brings us back to our illustration of a faithless England, where the church has been debilitated by the weak imitation of New Testament Christianity. Back to England, where "the church" is not the church, but stones and mortar; where the same *word* is used but where the reality is worlds apart. If for most British people "the church" means stained glass, steeples, and Sunday morning bells, for too many parachurch organizations it means sound stages, superstars, and satellites.

Christian media glitz is just the American revised version of King James stained glass. They share much in common. Glitz and stained glass permit us to *think* we are on the heavenly path without requiring us to walk a higher road. They allow us to confuse a fascination for the glorious with the true glory of a personal relationship with God.

Surely our human tendency to elevate the visible and the tangible over the invisible and intangible is at the heart of the difference between Christianity and the Jewish system of worship which it replaced. A look back at the attention given to the tabernacle and later to the temple stands in stark contrast to the simplicity of Christian worship. The importance of the transition was heralded by Jesus when he answered the Samaritan woman's question about whether God was to be worshiped in the mountains or in Jerusalem:

> . . . a time is coming and has now come
> when the true worshipers will worship the

Father in spirit and truth, for they are the kind
of worshipers the Father seeks. God is spirit,
and his worshipers must worship in spirit and
in truth (John 4:23,24).

Christianity's hallmark was the absence of temples,
altars, priests, and whatever else might permit the worshiper to miss the true spiritual implications of his
worship. Instead of *going* to a temple the worshiper *was*
the temple of God (1 Corinthians 3:16). Instead of ap-
proaching God *through* a priest he himself *became* a priest
(1 Peter 2:5,9). Instead of offering *animals* as sacrifices his
life was to be a daily sacrifice (Romans 12:1).

In every respect the New Testament church was a
radical departure from material manifestations of worship. There were no cathedrals or abbeys—just upper
rooms and meetings from house to house. There was no
stained glass to filter the light of daybreak—just the
enlightening light of the Word. There were no steeples
pointing heavenward—just Jesus' resurrection and ascen-
sion to say, "He will come again."

When Parachurch Parsons Fall

It is dangerous enough that we lose sight of what "the
church" is when we reduce it to mortar and brick,
stained glass and steeples. But we beg even greater
trouble when we overlay the church with the parachurch. Bricks and mortar are penny-ante compared
with ministries which require up to two million dollars a
month to survive.

Why do superstars in the church fall? Because too
often they are in fact superstars *outside* the church, in
parachurch organizations of their own making—in parachurch organizations where there is too much money,
too much power, and too much prestige for any mortal to
withstand.

The damage which can come from overemphasis on stained glass and steeples begins to look good when compared with the fall of just one parachurch superstar. What we've said before bears repeating: The more visible the leader, the more widespread the shame; the more prominent the leader, the greater the disgrace. The simple fact is that parachurch organizations by their very nature catapult their superstars into the public eye, visibly and prominently.

Misplaced Loyalty

On a visit to PTL more recent than the one I described earlier, I noted a new resolve for substance and integrity. Nevertheless, a staff member looked at the almost-empty Main Street at the Heritage Grand Hotel and lamented, "I can't believe how the [PTL] partners have abandoned this place. We have so much to accomplish, but they've allowed one man to ruin it all."

Abandonment seems to be the danger facing all parachurch ministries which depend for their existence on a superpersonality figurehead who falls. Because of the *minister*, people have left the *ministry*. What does that say about our allegiance to Christian ministries but that we give our money to men rather than to missions? This fact alone calls into question the wisdom of having parachurch organizations.

Sadly, PTL is convinced that it will take yet another superstar to bring in the money needed to operate its many programs. And PTL is not alone. When Pat Robertson left CBN to run for President, he took with him a large percentage of the donations which once supported "The 700 Club." The evidence is strong: For too many people, parachurch means media personality—not the Personhood of God.

Perhaps abandonment is what ought to happen if a ministry simply cannot survive without the presence of a superstar. Such a dilemma speaks volumes about how God intends his work to be accomplished. Or perhaps it is the fallen superstar alone who ought to be abandoned if the ministry remains true to its mission. Either way, abandonment is less likely when we are dealing with the church itself. In the church, the absence of any one man or woman should make very little difference. The ministry is God's. The church belongs to Christ. How could we ever abandon God's ministry and Christ's church?

God, bring us back into your church. Teach us again that, as the heavens are higher than the earth, so are your ways higher than our ways, and your thoughts than our thoughts. Let us guard ourselves when we walk the dangerous path of second-best, which time and again through the centuries has seduced the church away from the tasks you have given it and claimed the honor of those who lead your people.

Looking Within

- When scandals in parachurch ministries become the target of jokes, what is the impact on the church and on your personal ministry?
- What potential for scandal is lurking within your own life? Do other people have cause to laugh at your claim to be a Christian?
- How can you help to guard against scandal in the ministries and Christian colleges you support?
- If you are no longer supporting a ministry you once supported, is it because you have felt betrayed by its leader, or because you have lost faith in the mission of the ministry?
- Is your work and worship as a Christian tied more directly to a local church or to a parachurch ministry? What advantages for you might the church have over parachurch ministries?

9

From Soulmates
to Bedmates

The Pitfalls of Sexual Sin

There must have been more than 250 people at the Christian singles retreat that August. They ranged in age from young college kids to elderly grandmothers. Most were in their thirties and forties. A few had never been married, but most of them were widowed or divorced. Some were parents or grandparents, some were not. Women outnumbered men by a considerable number. I couldn't help but think that singleness was a fairly weak common denominator for such a diverse group. Sure enough, little subgroups started forming throughout the day—the younger, never-married college set; the middle-aged divorcees; and the older widows and widowers.

As I sat through the opening session, I wondered if maybe we had gotten it all wrong. In having "singles ministries," were we actually emphasizing even more than ever how different—almost odd—singles are? Instead of "singling" them out as a group, it occurred to me that maybe we could better channel our efforts into integrating single folks with married folks in the church.

By the time I had sorted all this out in my mind, I was somewhat put off again by the schedule of activities for the day. It was like attending a convention for the handicapped. The retreat topics verified that thought. For example, you could choose to attend classes on "Improving Your Self-Image" (are we assuming that all singles have a poor self-image?).

I chose to attend a class entitled "Sex and the Single

Christian," partly because it was a subject which interested me and partly because I was the teacher! My experience in speaking on this subject at other singles retreats led me to expect that my class would be filled to overflowing, which it was. However, it may have gotten more than usual promotion from the retreat Director. That morning, when announcing my 2:30 class, he got a rollicking response when he said, "LaGard Smith will be talking about sex in the afternoon!"

Put that way, I wasn't sure I was qualified to teach the class. But otherwise I was well-qualified. As a single person myself—under the heading of "never married"—and as a Christian committed in faith to the biblical teaching on sexual morality, I was well aware of the deadly minefield through which most single Christians walk each day. I had not come to speak as a neutral observer; I came as a fellow struggler.

Why is it that people so often choose to speak and write authoritatively about subjects with which they have difficulty in their own lives? The young woman who taught the class on self-assertiveness, for example, was a friend of mine whom I knew to be terribly insecure. Perhaps talking about it with other people is a way to deal with one's own problem. Perhaps it is because, having struggled with the problem, they've thought about it more than others and therefore have more to share.

The theme for my talk resulted from a personal study I had made about Christian sexuality. I had been particularly struck by a passage in 1 Corinthians chapter 6 in which Paul enigmatically tied together a discussion about sexual relations with a prostitute ("Do you not know that he who unites himself with a prostitute is one with her in body?") and language traditionally referring to the marriage relationship ("For it is said, 'The two will become one flesh.' "). As if that weren't sufficiently challenging, for good measure Paul added: "But he who unites himself with the Lord is one with him in spirit."

In the hour allotted to me, I drew from this and other passages to sketch out what I thought was a fresh approach to the subject of Christian sexuality. It called us away from the more obvious physical aspect of sexuality to our spirit-selves and how they interact. I described each of us as packages containing spirit-selves, pictured in my overhead transparencies something like Casper the Friendly Ghost in a box. Hugs, I suggested, were what take place when two spirit-selves share closeness and reach out to each other. The "packages" just get in between, that's all.

For me, the revolutionary thought coming out of 1 Corinthians chapter 6 was that in sexual intercourse two spirit-selves were not simply reaching out to each other, as in a hug, but that they in fact actually and literally intermingled! So much so that if one person's spirit-self were colored red, and the other's were colored blue, they each would take on a purple hue. Physical intimacy is even closer than we ever imagined!

This seemed to be the answer to the question I had always had as to the meaning of Paul's comment: "All other sins a man commits are outside his body, but he who sins sexually sins against his own body." I had always wondered why drunkenness and gluttony would not also have been sins against one's body. But Paul was talking about a particular abuse of the body which does something that no other sin does.

Sexual immorality literally joins a person spirit-to-spirit, with whomever he or she may be having sexual relations, whether it be a spouse, a lover, or—incredibly enough—even a prostitute! And it is because of this surprising fact that improper relations become sin. Joining another person spirit-to-spirit is wholly inappropriate outside the marriage relationship. When a couple goes through the motions of an act intended to bring about an intermingling of their spirit-selves, but without having committed their whole lives to each other, then sex becomes the ultimate self-deceiving masquerade.

Drawing the spiritual analogy between human marriage and our marriage to Christ, Paul shows how sexual immorality violates not only the trust of a spouse but also our commitment to Christ. "Do you not know that your bodies are members of Christ himself? Shall I then take the members of Christ and unite them with a prostitute?" Worse yet, sexual immorality threatens the very presence of the Holy Spirit, who also is intermingled intimately with us in our bodies: "Do you not know that your body is a temple of the Holy Spirit, who is in you, whom you have received from God? You are not your own; you were bought at a price. Therefore honor God with your body."

If I had understood Paul's teaching correctly, there was no such thing as "casual sex." Merely joining bodies would be one thing. But there's nothing casual about two people's spirit-selves being joined together as if one. For me, a whole new light had been shed on why we needed to struggle harder as single Christians to be spiritually pure. And I hoped that my new perspective would be of help to those in the room that day.

At the end of the hour a large number of those who had been in the class came up to express appreciation for new insight and renewed determination. It wasn't difficult to recognize the inner pain and sexual scars etched into the faces of one struggling Christian after another. Many happily-married Christians don't have the slightest idea what a battle it is for a single Christian to remain sexually pure in the midst of a sex-obsessed society.

But perhaps a lack of understanding runs both ways. When I see article after article by *married* spiritual leaders who fight sexual temptation and lose, I must admit I am mystified. I keep thinking that marriage should be a wonderful deliverance from the struggles of singleness.

A Close Encounter

As I put my notes into a folder and started to collect the transparencies from the overhead projector, I had that good feeling that always comes to me at the conclusion of a class that I think has gone well. After more than 15 years of teaching law, I still leave each class session on a "high." And when I have just finished a sermon or Bible class, the "high" is even higher. Why then should I have been surprised at what happened next?

"Hi, I'm Pam," I heard from over my shoulder. As I turned around, I saw an attractive young woman, dressed smartly, and with a well-worn Bible in hand. She continued, "I just wanted to tell you how wonderful your talk was. I've been divorced for two years, and I've really had to fight my need for physical companionship. Your presentation was exactly what I needed!" "I'm glad I could help in some way," I responded politely.

"I was particularly impressed with the way you helped me understand how sexuality is an extension of who we are spiritually. That was really at the heart of the problem with my ex-husband. He never understood me spiritually." I nodded understandingly. Then, reaching out to touch my arm, she said, "It's so wonderful to find a man who is spiritual."

It was then that I saw that look in her eye. That look I had seen at the door of the church building after giving a soul-baring sermon. That look which virtually every minister and Christian counselor reading this sentence has seen time after time. It was that "You're-the-spiritual-man-I've-needed-in-my-life" look.

I knew from experience that it was play-or-pass time. She was too physically attractive for the decision to be easy. She was too warm and affirming to immediately run out the door in the determined steps of Joseph running from Potiphar's wife. For the spiritual leader, special appreciation is heady wine. For the single person, special attention is intoxicating.

But this day I would be strong. This day I would cut right through the things about her which attracted me and see the hurting person she was within. She didn't need me, *as me*; she needed to feel deeply loved. She didn't need physical companionship; she needed feelings of security, appreciation, and understanding.

My guess was that she had pent-up feelings of rejection and self-doubt—perhaps even suffocating guilt. She was not unlike every other person who has experienced the pain of divorce. If I'm right about the literal intermingling of spirit-selves in sexual relations, then her divorce, just as literally, had ripped out half of who she had been.

We talked for awhile longer and shared the camaraderie of two strangers fighting a common enemy. But mutual vulnerability would not defeat us. It would only be a frightening reminder of that insidious force that can challenge one's deepest convictions at the very moment he has reaffirmed them to himself, and perhaps even to others.

An All-Too-Common Problem

Sexual vulnerability has always been an occupational hazard of spiritual leadership. In recognition of that fact, the Winter 1988 issue of *Leadership* magazine was dedicated to a discussion of sexual challenges to church leaders. It is "must reading" for every spiritual leader.

Leadership reports that 70 percent of pastors responding to a survey about pastoral indiscretion felt that spiritual leaders are "particularly vulnerable." It was disquieting to the editors to learn that 12 percent had committed adultery while they were in the ministry, and 23 percent had done something less than adulterous which they nevertheless acknowledged as "sexually inappropriate."

By contrast, a survey of nonpastors revealed a much

higher incidence of sexual sin: 23 percent participating in adultery and 45 percent acknowledging inappropriate sexual conduct. According to counselor David Mace, the happy surprise was that "for every pastor who has slipped on this icy surface, there are so many who have kept their balance."

The Special Taint of Sexual Sin

The scandals involving televangelists are reminders of the terrible consequences of sexual sin among spiritual leaders. One might speculate that in their cases it was the sin of pride which had led to relaxed moral restraint. But of course it was their sexual sin that brought down the house.

Sexual sins seem to be like speeding tickets: They are the only violations the public's radar is set to catch. It hardly matters that a driver who is going slower than the speed limit doesn't have a clue as to which lane of the road he is in, or doesn't yield the right-of-way to overtaking traffic, or is negligently engrossed in conversation with his passenger. If the alert driver in front of him goes over the speed limit, then it is he who will get the ticket.

It is the same with sexual sin. You can be sure that sexual sin will always get you busted. It hardly matters that at the top of Jesus' list of sins condemning spiritual leaders were the sins of arrogance and pride—both of which one can easily spot in pulpit after pulpit throughout the land, but which rarely, if ever, cause the dismissal of any spiritual leader.

Nor does it seem to matter whether the preacher repeatedly walked on the wild side, or fell only once in a moment of weakness. Whatever the individual case, sexual sin for the spiritual leader merits, in the minds of most people, nothing less than a professional death penalty.

I don't mean to diminish the impact of sexual sin in

the life of a spiritual leader. Sexual sin causes extraordinary disgrace outside the Christian community, despite the secular world's warped, double-standard hypocrisy. Sexual sin breaches trust with one's spouse, other church leaders, and the entire church. Sexual sin threatens the ability of a spiritual leader to counsel privately with others in the congregation. And sexual sin compromises the leader's ability to call people to higher responsibility in other areas of spiritual weakness.

Excitement or Escape?

With so much at risk, why would any spiritual leader—particularly a superstar of the Christian media—let himself get involved with sexual immorality? Have you ever thought that the risk itself might be the answer? If you have all the power and money you could ever hope for, perhaps sexual involvement—especially if it involves great risk—may bring excitement to one whose sense of excitement has been dulled by overachievement.

On the other hand, perhaps sex becomes just another way of escaping all the pressure at the top. It is perhaps the ultimate release. Like alcohol and drugs, sex can be the superstar's "outlet pass" when the media blitz is on. The difference may be that alcohol and drugs—and even addictive tendencies toward pornography—can be abused "in the closet," at times and places where the spiritual leader is all alone. But actual sexual misconduct requires the participation of another person, and thereby escalates the risk of public exposure.

Focusing on the sexual sins of a prominent televangelist may well mislead us as to the scope of the problem facing most spiritual leaders. We are not talking here about one or two bad apples in the barrel. For example, I think immediately of a widely read Christian author and lecturer across the Atlantic who has confided to a close friend that he has a great struggle with his carnal self.

And one could point to any number of highly respected ministers, teachers, and elders who have sexual skeletons in their closets. But why? How does it happen?

Temptations All Around

The brand of superstar sexual misconduct we have witnessed is not the typical shooting gallery through which the average spiritual leader walks. Nor, I suspect, are the hopefully-rare instances of "power-sex," which Paul instructed Timothy to beware of in unscrupulous spiritual leaders. "They are the kind," said Paul, "who worm their way into homes and gain control over weak-willed women, who are loaded down with sins and are swayed by all kinds of evil desires" (2 Timothy 3:6).

For the average spiritual leader it's the affair with the counselee who says, "If you really care about my needs, you'll hold me close." Or the minister who lets himself get emotionally involved with a woman sincerely seeking his spiritual guidance, discovering too late that their growing spiritual intimacy has opened the door to forbidden sexual expression.

As in all other workplaces, trouble may also come in the church office, with that sacrificial staff member who "understands" what the minister goes through, perhaps better than his own wife does. Or perhaps it is the vivacious young Sunday school teacher at the out-of-town Christian conference who made him laugh for the first time in ages. Or the woman in his own congregation whose sisterly hugs he always looks forward to with special anticipation.

From Spiritual to Sexual

Sexual temptations facing the spiritual leader are more deeply seated than normal, due to the very nature of sexuality. Because sex is tied with our spirit-selves, those whose business it is to nurture those spirit-selves are walking targets. *Leadership*'s managing editor, Marshall Shelley, explains the dynamic for us: "Though in distinct but parallel channels, spirituality and sexuality are separated by a wall thin enough for a strange osmosis to occur; the energies get mixed up."

When these conflicting feelings are put into close proximity, a sexual relationship can sneak up on both participants. Perhaps it started from a special closeness felt at a prayer session. As the prayer group joined hands in divine communication with God, the squeeze of hands communicated more than earnestness in prayer— and all quite innocently. But that closeness eventually developed to a point where each looked forward to the next prayer session for the wrong reasons. Fantasies appeared in the mind without warning, like a summer storm on the prairie.

Then came that accidental meeting—just the wrong place at just the wrong time—when the brotherly and sisterly hug unleashed a flood of feelings, including forbidden ones. The transference from spiritual to sexual had all but run its full course. Only by the grace of God would it stop there.

Many ministers and Christian counselors talk about experiencing a transference of feelings when discussing a counselee's sexual problems. What starts off to be a spiritual counseling session turns out to be an arousal of sexual feelings within the counselor himself. One might suggest that, rather than a transference of feelings, the arousal is the natural result of a kind of verbal voyeurism. One can hardly underestimate the dangerous potential within the walls of a church office should this transference occur.

Transference can work the other way around as well. A counselee can find herself transferring her desire for God to the "man of God" who sits there before her. But this transference has all the makings of a time bomb. If the spiritual leader ever steps out of his idealized role and pursues the counselee sexually, she is likely to turn that disillusioned betrayal into well-warranted angry retaliation.

Contributing Causes

There are other dynamics besides transference which contribute to sexual falls among spiritual leaders. One is the "Hothouse syndrome," where good Christian kids from good Christian homes go to good Christian colleges in order to become good Christian spiritual leaders, only to be shoved out into a not-so-good secular world full of temptations from which the fledgling spiritual leaders have been protected all their lives. Given their sheltered existence, it is no wonder that so many of them wilt under the worldly temptations they encounter.

Another contributor is the kind of loneliness that only a spiritual leader can know. The "Elijah syndrome" goes something like this: "Lord, I have been very zealous for the cause of Christ. The people in my congregation have rejected their spiritual responsibilities, broken good spiritual habits, and killed any efforts which I have made to bring them back to you. I am the only one left, and now they are after my job too" (see 1 Kings 19:10).

You stand up for principles that seem irrelevant to other people. You insist on doing biblical things in biblical ways, but nobody seems to care. You spend your whole life concerned about the spiritual growth of the church while everyone else fusses about the color of the sanctuary. You talk about the need to visit the sick but find yourself alone at the hospital. You preach social justice but can't get anyone to go with you to visit inmates in the county jail. After years of ministry you can find yourself terribly alone. And if there's not an understanding shoulder at home, there are other shoulders to be found.

When Elijah felt the loneliness of spiritual leadership, he went into a cave and spent the night. Lesser spiritual leaders have gone into other dark places and spent the night.

Still another contributor is the "Not-Me syndrome." For some reason, many spiritual leaders seem to assume they are invulnerable to sexual temptation. Launching themselves with that kind of Titanic attitude puts them at great risk when they enter the chilly waters of ministry. Paul himself had experienced the "Not-Me syndrome," only to be brought up short by a God who cried out to him on the Damascus road, "Saul, Saul, why do you persecute me?" He knew the false confidence of self-righteousness. Therefore it was surely from the depths of his own experience that he wrote, "So, if you think you are standing firm, be careful that you don't fall!" (1 Corinthians 10:12).

No wonder, too, that Paul was so emphatic in his anticipatory warning to the young evangelist, Timothy: "Treat younger men as brothers, older women as mothers, and younger women as sisters, with absolute purity" (1 Timothy 5:1,2). Surely Paul had no reason to distrust Timothy. But he also knew how easy it is for anything less than *absolute* purity to bring down even the strongest spiritual leader.

One last contributor to the problem, the "Somebody-Loves-Me syndrome," is a surprise entry. Pride has so often been the serpent in the grass pointing the way to sexual impropriety that we might never suspect one's fall could come from the opposite end of the garden. But the evidence is clear: Many leaders have fallen in an attempt to bolster *deflated* egos.

Not all spiritual leaders are egocentric. In fact, more than we might suspect are nurturing inferiority complexes. If they haven't brought inferiority feelings with them into the ministry, then they easily acquire them once the inevitable criticism starts flowing in their direction. Trying to please all of the people all of the time is one of the most frustrating jobs of the local spiritual leader.

Enter, stage left, the rescuing, sympathetic, ego-feeding, mission-affirming godly woman he searches out in the congregation. Exit, stage right, the virtue, reputation, and position of yet another fallen leader.

Avoiding the Temptation

I like very much the approach of Randy Alcorn, of Good Shepherd Community Church in Gresham, Oregon. "In the wake of several Christian leaders' falling into immorality, a co-pastor and I developed a list of specific consequences that would result from our immorality."

Fear has not always gotten the best press as a spiritual motivation, but it does have scriptural backing. Solomon, himself a fallen leader, wrote: "The fear of the Lord is the beginning of knowledge, but fools despise wisdom and discipline" (Proverbs 1:7). And Jesus pulled no punches about the eternal consequences we face when he warned, "Be afraid of the one who can destroy both soul and body in hell" (Matthew 10:28).

The more immediate consequences are almost as frightening. Alcorn's list included, for example, inflicting hurt on his wife and family, and perhaps losing them altogether; wasting years of ministry training; losing self-respect; forfeiting years of witnessing to others about coming to Christ; hurting the illicit sexual partner; and invoking lifelong shame and embarrassment.

If anything good can come out of recent sexual scandals, perhaps it is the spine-chilling thought of what can happen if the walls of our own house crumble around us.

I like Alcorn's style in avoiding temptation: "Once I was undergoing a time of strong sexual temptation," writes Alcorn, "and finally I called a friend with whom I was having breakfast the next day. I said, 'Please pray for me, and ask me tomorrow morning what I did.' " Now that's a clever way to achieve accountability!

Others have said that spiritual leaders must form the habit of including their wives in the defense against temptation. "Talk with them about the temptations which you think may lurk along your path that day," they suggest.

For Christian counselors, there is this special advice: When possible, keep the office door open. "Behind closed doors" is a phrase packing a great potential for trouble in all sorts of areas. When privacy simply cannot be avoided, call in a team member. And if that isn't possible, at least let someone know why the door is being shut. What an unlikely enemy a door is—but sometimes our reputations can hinge on it!

The flip side of that coin draws the advice "Stay at the office." Private meetings over lunch, or at some other out-of-the-way place, can be a source of both temptation and unnecessary rumor. Rumors have a funny way of starting, even in the most innocent of situations. A colleague of mine who had recently undergone a separation from his wife was seen having lunch with an "attractive young thing." Rumors spread rapidly, until it was finally disclosed that the "attractive young thing" was his 18-year-old daughter!

Kisses, Hugs, and Handshakes

The apostle Paul may have commented indirectly on a whole new set of problems when he urged first-century Christians to "Greet one another with a holy kiss" (1 Corinthians 16:20). Of course, we recognize that his emphasis was on the word "holy." The Corinthians would already have been greeting each other with a kiss—in the same first-century manner that Judas kissed

Jesus, and in the same manner that many societies, even today, employ the kiss as a customary greeting. In our culture the kiss has become a handshake, although increasingly in the church the handshake is being replaced by a hug.

At the University Church on the campus where I teach, we are mostly "huggers." Our former university president and now elder statesman, Dr. Howard White, seems to get more than his share from admiring coeds. It's the grandfather image, you know. And the young campus ministers are never far from a hug. But the rest of us, too, are rarely lacking for a brotherly or sisterly arm around the shoulder.

Hugs are one of the little joys in life which tell us we are important. They are warm and loving, and they often express the special fellowship that only Christians can know. But because hugs can be interpreted in so many different ways—some good, some bad—hugs present the spiritual leader with yet another potential path to danger. It ought to be obvious, but carefully monitoring "holy hugs" should be part of the spiritual leader's daily battle plan for self-defense.

Marriage and family therapist Andre Bustanoby puts hugs in perspective. "We have to be totally honest with ourselves," he writes. "Do we touch (physically or verbally) out of sexual attraction, out of an inner desire to exploit the situation, or do we touch out of a spontaneous expression of care for that person, quite apart from gender?"

Even Solomon said, "There is a time to embrace and a time to refrain." We *do* know the difference, don't we? Here's to more hugs. Here's to more *holy* hugs.

The Christian Challenge

Like many other people, I too have asked, "Why didn't the Bible give us some insight as to how *Jesus* dealt with his sexuality? What did *he* do when a sensuously beautiful Palestinian woman walked by? What did *he* feel when he approached the sexually experienced Samaritan woman at the well? How did *he* react when women in vulnerable circumstances sought out his spiritual strength?

What we *do* know is that Christ always looked past the flesh into the heart and soul of a person. So because the woman who washed his feet with her hair was a troubled and lost person, that is all that Jesus saw. Because the woman at the well had been loved and left, time and again, it was only her inner hurt that Jesus saw. With his focus on the inner person, Jesus was free from the temptations associated with the outer person.

How do men and women of God suddenly find themselves involved in sexual sin? The same way as anyone else—by looking with the wrong perspective, then yielding to lust and letting it take control of their actions.

Forget the psychological analysis and interesting pastoral theories we talked about earlier. Forget the pressures which all spiritual leaders have but which act as excuses for only a few. Forget the part that other people may play in the process of seduction. The bottom line is fleshly desire uncontrolled. Fleshly desire unpurged. Fleshly desire allowed to have its way. That is the point where we must triumph.

Understanding how sexual temptation likely will come our way is helpful. Gaining insight into the overlapping dynamics of spirituality and sexuality is a first-line defense. But at the fork in the road we are faced with nothing less than a battle between flesh and spirit. And only we ourselves are responsible for that decision. No theories. No excuses. No blaming. No rationalizations.

How do spiritual leaders fall sexually? The same way as everybody else who sins sexually—by keeping that part of their lives within their own sovereignty. By consciously allowing their sexual selves to triumph over their spiritual selves.

When all is said and done, there will always be the battle between spirit and flesh. The world would think us crazy to ever even try to keep ourselves pure. But God has called us to come out and be separate. "Be holy, as I am holy" is the challenge.

Why do spiritual leaders fall sexually? Because we minister daily in God's temples but forget that our own bodies are the temples in which his Holy Spirit dwells. Lord, so fill us with your holiness that we will not give place to the pernicious desires which seduce our carnal selves.

Looking Within

- Why do you suppose scandals involving spiritual leaders so often involve sexual sin?
- If you feel particularly vulnerable to sexual sin, what steps can you take to help you win the battle?
- Who can you turn to for help when you face sexual temptations? Have you sought God's strength through prayer?
- What do you have to lose if you fall to sexual sin?
- If you do not feel particularly vulnerable to sexual sin, are there ways in which you have left yourself open for reputation-ruining rumors or even an unexpected fall?

10

Good Man of God, Bad Man of God

The Struggles of Spiritual Warfare

In Nathaniel Hawthorne's great American classic, *The Scarlet Letter*, the Reverend Mr. Arthur Dimmesdale was "considered by his more fervent admirers as little less than a heaven-ordained apostle." Unfortunately, Hawthorne's "heaven-ordained apostle," a bachelor, fell into the arms of young Hester Prynne, and from there into sin. A child was born of their illicit liaison, but for years Dimmesdale's paternity was known only to Hester.

One might have thought that eventually Dimmesdale's private fall would have been absorbed into the backroads of his consciousness. However, that was never to be. He simply could not live with either the guilt or with what he perceived to be the hypocrisy of his hallowed position as a man of God. For seven years he struggled to serve his congregation honorably, despite deteriorating health and sanity.

Then came the day when Dimmesdale could bear the pain no longer. At a forest rendezvous with Hester, he bares the agonizing turmoil within his soul.

> What can a ruined soul, like mine, effect towards the redemption of other souls?—or a polluted soul, towards their purification? And as for the people's reverence, would that it were turned to scorn and hatred. Canst thou deem it, Hester, a consolation, that I must

stand up in my pulpit, and meet so many eyes turned upward toward my face, as if the light of heaven were beaming from it!—must see my flock hungry for the truth, and listening to my words as if a tongue of Pentecost were speaking!—and then look inward, and discern the black reality of what they idolize? I have laughed in bitterness and agony of heart, at the contrast between what I seem and what I am! And Satan laughs at it!

When no satisfactory avenue for venting his raging guilt readily manifested itself, Dimmesdale shocked his congregation by making a public confession of the sin which had so easily beset him, and which had so doggedly dragged him into the depths of despair. Even in the face of fearful consequences, this broken man of God could hide no longer from his own self-condemnation.

Spiritual Dissonance

Had there been a psychologist sitting around somewhere in 1850, he might have analyzed Dimmesdale's problem as "cognitive dissonance." I see that term floating around occasionally now, but I'll never forget the first time I ever heard it. It was the title and theme of a sermon my father once preached. I remember being particularly struck by the term, because it wasn't like Dad to use it. Although Dad was well-read, he rarely pulled out "highfalutin words," as he might have put it.

Dad's sermon pointed to the spiritual battle within each of us when we believe one way and act another. It is Paul's "dissonance" when he did what he knew he ought not to do. It is Peter's "dissonance" when he wept bitterly after denying Christ. It is *our* "dissonance" when we find ourselves having done something that is completely out of character for us.

A spiritual leader may also sense dissonance in his life when his battle is in the conflicting motivations of his heart, even though he may not have acted upon his baser impulses. In his book *Christ in the Seasons of Ministry*, John Killinger tells of a conversation with a highly respected minister of a large, prestigious church. When the minister was asked what thoughts ran through his mind as he entered the last phase of his ministry, the surprising response was: "Sex and love." The minister went on to explain:

> "I've had a devil of a time with sex these last few years," he said; "wanta put my arm around every attractive woman I see. Put my arm around her—I want to get into bed with her. I haven't. But I've sure had the urge.
>
> "By love," he said, "I mean this." He waved his hand in a semisweep, indicating the extremely large church building completed within the last five years. "I used to think that the ultimate was to build this building. You know, the old edifice complex. Now that it's built, I think a lot about love. What good is a building if the people aren't changed? I'd like to spend the rest of my ministry teaching people how to love."

Can you think of a more vivid example of dissonance in the life of a spiritual leader? His thoughts ran with alternate swiftness between wanting to bed the women in his congregation and wanting to teach his congregation how to love! How do you suppose he reconciled the chasm between his physical self and his spiritual self? Even more intriguing, perhaps—would any of the members of his congregation ever have guessed his spiritual schizophrenia? What if they had?

Special Dissonance for Special People

Cognitive dissonance—what the Bible refers to as spiritual warfare—is a relentless predator in the mind of every Christian. It hounds us, plagues us, and never leaves us alone. It hangs around just to remind us of our fallibility. Perhaps it is simply a highfalutin term for "conscience," with which each of us is thankfully endowed. Were it not for conscience, we probably would never even engage the enemy.

However, for the spiritual leader, spiritual dissonance bears a greater burden. As with Arthur Dimmesdale, countless spiritual leaders sink into debilitating guilt and inner conflict. We think of these leaders as being warm, sensitive, giving, righteous, pure, and godly. They think of themselves as great sinners, unworthy of the positions which they hold. We may be shocked occasionally at the spiritual shortcomings of a spiritual leader, but they live in an ongoing state of shock at the thought of who they really are.

The young, earnest preacher preaches his heart out with the message of the gospel. His congregation grows. A new, bigger building is built. Perhaps he is asked to speak across the nation or to appear on radio and television. His name becomes well-known. He is showered with attention. He is a celebrity. Then one day it dawns on him that he is posing. Posing, not preaching. He's preaching one message but living another.

"With Jesus you can control your anger," he proclaims boldly from the pulpit. But at home he yells at his wife. "With Jesus you can overcome depression," he says glibly in Sunday's sermon. But on Monday he is wallowing in depression. "With Jesus you can overcome temptation" is his confident assurance to hundreds of faces in the audience. But when he looks at his own face in the mirror, he knows he has fallen prey to temptation more times than he can remember.

It doesn't take long before the preacher has convinced himself that he is a fake. It doesn't take long for him to doubt the power of his message. It doesn't take long for all his youthful idealism to be exploded. And it is then that alienation sets in, and isolation and guilt consume him. It is then that he is cut loose from his moorings and is vulnerable to drifting away.

Someone might say, "But preachers and elders are the ones who know God best. Why don't they pray for strength? If consumed with guilt, why don't they pray for forgiveness, accept God's grace, and then get on with their lives?" The answer may lie in the very type of people we are apt to find as religious leaders. They are indeed caring people—so much so that they really care about sin, particularly in their own lives. They are indeed sensitive individuals—so much so that they are crushed by sin when others would barely be bruised.

There is this to think about as well, although the categorization may be excessively encompassing: Those who study the relationship between personality traits and occupations tell us some very interesting things about ourselves. If the experts are to be believed, those who go into law, for example, have an inordinate need for order in their lives; those who enter into medicine, an inordinate fear of death. They confirm as fact what many have jokingly said—that psychiatrists are indeed unusually burdened with emotional struggles of their own.

I have not seen an analysis of the dominant personality trait leading to spiritual leadership, but one could speculate, with at least some confirmation, that many who enter the ministry are people burdened with an acute awareness of sin in their lives. Perhaps it relates to the observation that people often end up talking authoritatively about problems which they themselves encounter to a greater degree than others.

To the extent that people end up as spiritual leaders precisely because they struggle more than others with sin—or rather because they are more *affected* than others by their sin—then cognitive dissonance is to be expected of them. They have made a career out of dissonance. Even if many others are drawn to ministry by a call of God, they too will come to know the inner struggle of the sinner called to a position of righteous leadership.

For those who keenly feel the personal battles of spiritual warfare, there is rarely any comfort in knowing that they are not alone. Paul's confessed conflicts, or Peter's inner shame, come as little consolation. Sin in the life of a spiritual leader is a personal mountain to be climbed, no matter how many others have worn down the well-traveled path of penance. And even when refreshment is sought at the natural spring along the way, the question on the sign is a disheartening reminder: "Can both fresh water and salt water flow from the same spring?" (James 3:11).

Too-Great Expectations

Of course, the chief enemy of the dissonant spiritual leader is unrealistic expectations—both his own and those of the people who look to him for leadership. It is difficult to judge which expectation is more fearsome.

The expectations of others can push perfection to the limit. With the rest of us there is a margin for error, but for the recognized spiritual leader there is only strict liability. For the rest of us, being tripped up by sin makes us "human." But for the spiritual leader, being tripped up by sin and immorality means the loss of everything.

In a brilliant British detective television series, the star of the show, Chief Inspector Morse, muses about a priest who succumbed to temptation and never recovered from the experience. Then Morse turns to his partner and says haltingly, with a reflective grimace, "That's what we do to clergymen. We expect to see Christ through them . . . and they wilt under it."

The Invasion of Privacy

Living in a glass house under constant scrutiny has always been as much an invitation to moral failure as the deterrent which one might expect the public nature of a spiritual leader's open life to be. If the openness of a leader's life compels public displays of right conduct, it also chases one into the shadows in search of privacy and one's own humanity. And it is in that darkened alley leading to freedom from scrutiny that many a spiritual leader has tripped and fallen.

In modern times the problem of the spiritual leader's dual personality—the kind of person he is when leading in public and who he is in private—has intensified. With the media explosion, both in sheer volume (the number of books, articles, cable stations, and reporters on the streets) and quality (now, typically, *investigative* reporting), there has come to leaders of all kinds a feeling that "big brother is watching." No longer is the political or spiritual leader able to find sufficient space to deal with the inevitable ebbs and flows of his own spiritual life in a private way.

If it is a good thing that a highly recognized spiritual leader cannot cruise motel row with impunity, ironically it may also have contributed to the very reason he was there in the first place. Without in any way excusing such conduct, it is important to consider that today's interrogation-level public scrutiny may in fact drive some leaders to radical and inappropriate behavior (sin) to escape what seems like unfair attention, to escape a crowding of one's personal life.

What makes good men and women fall into sin? For some, the spotlight of constant surveillance drives them underground, where they have no business going.

Pushing Ourselves Beyond Reasonable Expectations

Quite apart from the expectations of other people, personal expectations can push one even further, perhaps to the breaking point. With the rest of us, sin is cause for forgiveness and renewed dedication. But for the spiritual leader, sin is confirmation of one's total unworthiness as "a guide for the blind and a light for those who are in the dark." The rest of us are content to be "human," striving to be more and more righteous. But the spiritual leader feels he must be superhuman from start to finish.

Why do spiritual leaders crack before we know what is happening? Because, like us, they are only human. And because sometimes both we and they forget that fact.

Isn't it odd that the conscientious spiritual leader goes around feeling like a hypocrite when he ministers to others—knowing that he himself is not perfect—while spiritual leaders who never think about it that way are the real hypocrites?

Even if we think of a preacher as one of the most righteous men we have ever known, in the back of our minds we are never fooled. We know that, regardless of whatever sterling character he may have, ultimately he cannot help but say to us: "Do as I say, not as I do." Only Jesus Christ could have said, "Do as I say, *and* as I do." Where some preachers cross the line is in pretending otherwise.

Hypocrisy is not the proper charge for imperfect preachers, or else every spiritual leader would be a hypocrite. It is the person who screams and shouts about others being involved in the same sins with which he knows he is condemned who is the true hypocrite. In that kind of self-righteous high-handedness there is *callous* cognitive dissonance. No, that's too cute a term. The proper label is arrogant hypocrisy!

Paul scathingly rebuked that kind of hypocritical dissonance. Even though he obviously was addressing the

Judaizing teachers of his time, one gets the feeling that Paul has been reading recent headlines:

> ...you, then, who teach others, do you not teach yourself? You who preach against stealing, do you steal? You who say that people should not commit adultery, do you commit adultery? You who abhor idols, do you rob temples? You who brag about the law, do you dishonor God by breaking the law? As it is written: "God's name is blasphemed among the Gentiles because of you" (Romans 2:21-24).

This is a call for humility in preaching. It is a call for less shouting and more tears—genuine tears. It is a call for confessional preaching, where the preacher leaves the lofty pretentiousness of the pulpit and mingles with the audience as a fellow sinner.

But it would be too self-serving if the lesson stopped there. Paul is telling us more than simply how we ought to preach to others, whatever the volume level and however many tears are in the eyes. His rebuke is a call for spiritual leaders to practice what they preach—if imperfectly, at least more and more each day. It is a call for personal growth, where the preacher steps away from his congregation and launches out ahead toward the lofty heights of true righteousness. Enough of mediocre fraternalism! Bring on the spiritual giants!

Why do spiritual leaders get into trouble? Because, as with the rest of us, it is too easy for them to say, "But I'm only human, after all. What do you expect—perfection?" No, we don't demand perfection, but neither should we be asked to accept cop-outs.

If our humanity can become our downfall because other people demand more than we can deliver, our humanity can also be a trap for cheap grace. Yes, we are only human, but God calls us toward perfection through his grace: "Be perfect, therefore, as your Father in heaven is perfect" (Matthew 5:48). Perfected sinners is the goal. Perfected sinners is who we must strive to be.

Two Sides Are Better Than One

If only we could grasp a proper perspective. Spiritual leaders are undoubtedly never as righteous as their friends might believe them to be, nor as unrighteous as their enemies might hope. Like the rest of humanity, spiritual leaders are both good and bad. And for me there is a hidden blessing in that fact. Their spiritual schizophrenia plays well into the hands of my own dilemma about preachers.

When I think of who I want for a preacher, I sometimes want a man who has no sins, so that his message of moral purity and eternal judgment is never diminished by his own life. The church needs righteous role models and uncompromising teachers. If there is a drunken Noah, a lying Abraham, and an adulterous David in the Bible, there is also a righteous Enoch, a pure Elijah, and an obedient Ezekiel. And, oh, how I would love to listen to a sermon by Daniel or Ezra!

On the other hand, I also want a preacher who is just as sinful as I am, so that I can know his message of grace is personally felt. Send me Noah, and Abraham, and David. I want to know how they were lifted up by God's mercy and forgiveness. The church needs men in the pulpit who understand the sins of those who sit in the pew.

But how can the same man be both?

One hardly need make a case for the virtue of having virtuous leaders. Virtuous leadership is what we have every right to expect from those who assume the mantle of leadership. And "virtuous" is what God calls spiritual leaders to be. But I believe there is also a case to be made for the virtue of fallenness among those who lead us. If that seems to be a fairly radical thought, perhaps it is because we have more fallenness than we know what to do with these days.

However, I propose that when spiritual leaders fall they fall headlong into a grand design. Steady now—I'm not suggesting that God trips up good men in order to carry out his purposes. What I *am* suggesting is that God turns even fallenness into part of his plan. Paul suggests as much when he speaks of the difference between the gospel message and those who are called to proclaim that message:

> We do not preach ourselves, but Jesus Christ as Lord, and ourselves as your servants for Jesus' sake. For God, who said, "Let light shine out of darkness," made his light shine in our hearts to give us the light of the knowledge of the glory of God in the face of Christ.
>
> But we have this treasure in jars of clay to show that this all-surpassing power is from God and not from us (2 Corinthians 4:5-7).

Fallen spiritual leaders may be God's built-in method of keeping his *message* supreme.

If spiritual leaders were perfect, then we would tend to worship them. But since Jesus alone is perfect, then the message of hope that points us to him must remain paramount. Those who proclaim the gospel message are but clay jars, cracked and broken. What they bring to us is exquisite and faultless, but they themselves are anything but that.

The wonder is that God can turn the fallenness of spiritual leaders into a blessing for others. Here's to spiritual leaders who teach not only from the pure waters of biblical truths but also from the muddy waters of broken lives brought back to Christ. Here's to preachers who bring us sermons not only from dedicated study of the Bible but also from struggles within the heart. Here's to elders who counsel not only with the power of the written Word but also with the transcendence of personal experience. Here's to Bible class teachers who not only prepare their lessons prayerfully and carefully but who also dare to share the lessons of their own vulnerability.

Praise God for blessing us with righteous men and women of faith, who have always followed their calling with moral exactitude. And praise God for fallen leaders who can both point the way through teaching and show us the way through personal examples of having overcome moral weakness.

The Great Paradox

Having just presented a case for the ultimate good that can come from the fallenness of spiritual leaders, I am forced immediately to the other side of the coin. Even though the members of the congregation want to know that they have spiritual leaders who struggle with temptation and sin as they do, they are not anxious to *hear* about it. It is the preacher's paradox. "Be weak if you must," says the person in the pew, "but don't give us the details. Let us know that you are a fellow struggler, but don't let yourself come down to our level!" And isn't that reaction right on the money? If there is no one we can look up to spiritually, then why have spiritual leaders?

It is somewhat like parents who suspect what their children may be doing wrong, but will do everything in the world to avoid knowing for sure. Or the wife who wonders if her husband may be having an affair, but can't stand the thought of asking for the truth. It's all those times when someone says, "Don't tell me. I don't want to know about it."

We once had a preacher who thought it was an act of humility to reveal his inner struggles—explicitly. He didn't last very long. It wasn't that we would not have allowed his weaknesses, but when he kept throwing them in our face, the natural reaction was, "Why should we listen to you? Our sins are starting to look pretty good alongside yours!"

I must point you to an excellent article by Alice Poynor, a homemaker and free-lance Christian writer. In asking "Where Have All the Heroes Gone?" (*Christianity Today*, September 1984), Poynor suggests that we may have gone overboard with the trendy words "identify," "relate," "honesty," and "realism." She tells of a scene she once witnessed, which for me—in light of the preacher I just told you about—was déjà vu:

> A minister visiting in another church was chatting with a group of believers in various stages of Christian maturity. He spilled out the failings, the doubts he feels, and yes, the sins to which he falls prey—even now as a pastor. Each succeeding revelation seemed calculated to cast aspersion, not only on himself, but on the ministry he represents. "I think it's best to be honest," he told them. "Preachers aren't any better than the rest of you, you know."

Poynor then recalled a number of people who had been spiritual giants as she grew up in the Lord. Their bigger-than-life examples had always been an encouragement to her. "Oh, of course they sinned. We knew that. Nor would any of us really believe our minister to be sinless, or a beloved Bible teacher to be above temptation. But we hardly get a blessing from knowing about their sins. We know our neighbors must accumulate garbage, too, but we appreciate them hiding it behind the fence."

There are other dangers as well, graphically seen as Poynor completes the thought picture: "Christian love demands that we don't line up our garbage cans where our brother will trip over them. (Or worse, that we don't come to accept trash as beautiful just because everyone on the block has some.)"

Seductive Rationalization

I've always liked the picture which Isaiah painted of "those who draw sin along with cords of deceit, and wickedness as with cart ropes" (Isaiah 5:18). What a wonderful description of rationalization in motion: Sin, with all its burden, easily drawn along with just a thin string of self-deception!

Frankly, I suspect that "honest confession" by spiritual leaders can be a convenient way to pull along truckloads of sin. The author of an article I once read about so-called "victimless crimes" observed that we have any number of crimes on the books, like gambling and prostitution, to which we give only token enforcement. His explanation? We feel better about going ahead and participating in questionable activities if we have at least denounced that conduct in our laws!

Likewise, it is easy for someone to rationalize his sin by saying to himself, "I'm no longer a hypocrite, because I have revealed my sin to those I lead. Since *they* have continued to accept me, *I too* can continue to accept me (the way I am, without needing to change)."

Spiritual leaders can also sometimes be the very best at a game that lots of other people play—the "Only-One-Weakness" game. Once again, my friend Jim McGoldrick says it well in his essay on David:

> David could move from adultery to deceit to murder so quickly. We may think that we can choose just one sin, just one failure, just one

shortcoming, and preserve our other values. That is almost never the case. The forgoing of our values, the giving up of what we know to be right, in one area leads progressively and quickly to deterioration of values in other areas.

It is impossible to draw lines, to stop sin within a certain controlled environment. That just never works. The choice to do wrong in one area will build in every area and infect the whole of life.

If sin can sometimes be turned into a blessing for others, the rationalization of sin never can, especially on the part of a spiritual leader. How do you suppose big-name televangelists had managed for so long to rationalize their sins? Probably with the same inventiveness as the rest of us. We are all far too clever for our own good.

To Whom Shall We Turn?

What we want are spiritual leaders who are acutely aware of their own fallenness but who don't advertise "Film at eleven." That sounds fair enough; what more could spiritual leaders want? We're allowing them to struggle with temptation behind the scenes, as long as they don't hang their dirty linen on a line from one wall to another across the church building.

Sure, that sounds reasonable, but by no means does it solve the problem. In fact, it *becomes* the problem!

The president of a college I attended is a great storyteller. He once told about the minister who played hooky from Sunday morning worship in order to get in 18 holes of golf. On the sixteenth hole the minister wound up and let the club fly. The ball took off on a beeline for the green, hit the pole, and dropped neatly into the cup. When the minister got to the green and discovered he had just hit the only hole-in-one of his life, he fell to his knees and began crying with loud sobs. The clouds darkened, lightning pierced the sky, and a thundering voice from heaven said, "My son, why are you crying? You just hit a hole-in-one. I thought it would make you happy." The minister, looking up with surprise and embarrassment, said, "But who can I tell?"

That's always the problem when a spiritual leader "plays hooky" from his moral commitments—"Who can I tell?" If there is a spouse about the house, perhaps the problem is solved. But only perhaps. What if the sin would hurt rather than help the marriage? (I'll leave it to those more qualified to sort out when you tell and when you don't.) But suppose that, for whatever reason, this option is unavailable?

It came in a different context altogether, but Peter's question is still the question being asked by fallen spiritual leaders: "Lord, to whom shall we turn?" (The implication, by the way, was an affirmation that in the last analysis the only one to whom we truly can turn is Jesus Christ himself.)

And the question of who we can go to for counsel and advice ought to be asked with all due deliberation, knowing that a wrong choice could spell irreversible disaster. Everywhere one turns there are risks that confidences will be betrayed. Even when you tell your best friends, you can never be certain that what you have said will not surface—sometime, someplace. There need be nothing malicious about the way it gets out. It just gets out, like the proverbial cat out of the proverbial bag.

Of course the revelation of disclosed confidences can indeed be the result of malicious opportunism. Recently, as we are all too well aware, a strange mixture of mutual concern and political rivalry among Christian media superstars accounted for much private talk going public. Yet with even the minor power struggles going on within smaller ministries and local churches, many spiritual leaders feel they are simply at too great a risk to speak openly about their struggles with sin. The supportive elder this year may be the very one to play the trump card of your confession next year.

Even if confidences are never betrayed, there are other hidden risks in baring your soul to someone else. There is, for example, the risk that you might become isolated from friends to whom your exposure would constitute a political liability. They may back away from you as if you were literally plagued by your sin.

It must be pointed out that the shoe is not always on the other fellow's foot. Sometimes there is hesitancy on the part of the fallen leader himself, despite the availability of those who would lend sympathetic and confidential ears. Hesitancy to talk with others about one's sins is as natural as a child who wouldn't dare disclose personal foibles to his parents. The same concern may operate with a spouse, the very one with whom you ought to be able to share everything.

This hesitancy is not a matter of being secretive or dishonest. Rather, it is a matter of respect for those you love most. It is a respect that says, "*I'm* already hurting, and I don't want to hurt *you*, too," or, "I don't want you to have to bear the burden of my sin; I love you too much to ask you to do that."

So where do we turn? The "Greyhound Bus syndrome" might work in the rare instance. You know, those times when you meet a perfect stranger—on a bus, or a train, or a plane—and you tell him things you wouldn't tell your best friend. It's safe. Who is he going to tell that would matter at all? Unfortunately, the problem is that most strangers wouldn't understand a person's spiritual struggles even if they were otherwise sympathetic.

So the spiritual leader faces a difficult dilemma indeed. And if there is simply no one he can turn to for consolation and support, the cycle of sin may be prolonged or even deepened.

Of course, many fallen leaders struggling with unsharable secret sin will indeed turn their faces steadfastly to God in prayer. Whether King David had those with whom he could bare the unbearable we are not told. But from his poignant psalms of contrition I get the feeling that—king though he was—he may have had only God in his corner.

Who can ever forget Psalm 51, the ultimate anguished plea of a spiritual leader fallen into sin? If ever there was a man of God who knew the pain of spiritual dissonance or the loneliness of undeserved spiritual leadership, it was David. His agonizing prayer has been the prayer of every conscientious person of God who has ever faced his or her own unworthiness:

> Have mercy on me, O God,
>   according to your unfailing love;
> according to your great compassion
>   blot out my transgressions.
> Wash away all my iniquity
>   and cleanse me from my sin.
>
> For I know my transgressions,
>   and my sin is always before me.
> Against you, you only, have I sinned
>   and done what is evil in your sight....
>
> Cleanse me with hyssop, and I will be clean;
>   wash me, and I will be whiter than
>   snow....
>
> Create in me a pure heart, O God,
>   and renew a steadfast spirit within me.
> Do not cast me from your presence
>   or take your Holy Spirit from me.

Restore me to the joy of your salvation
and grant me a willing spirit, to
sustain me. . . .

You do not delight in sacrifice, or I would
bring it; you do not take pleasure in burnt
offerings.
The sacrifices of God are a broken spirit;
a broken and contrite heart,
O God, you will not despise.

Whether it be King David, Hawthorne's Arthur Dimmesdale, Jimmy Swaggart, or you and I, Psalm 51 is the sublime expression of broken contrition for all of us who have ever experienced the spiritual dissonance of being good men and women of God, bad men and women of God. May God bring us ever closer into being just one person. *His* person.

Looking Within

- What is the spiritual dissonance you feel in your life? Can you think of ways to bring your "dual personality" into closer harmony through Christ?
- Whose expectations do you feel most keenly the need to live up to—the expectations of others, your own expectations, or God's?
- Are there ways in which inconsistencies between your spiritual self and your carnal self actually amount to hypocrisy?
- Do you rationalize the sin in your life by assuring yourself that you have "just one major weakness"?
- Do you already have a support partner or someone in whom you can confide? If not, is there someone you can turn to in your church?

11

Forgiving, Forgetting, Forbearing

The Problem of Restoration

By now you may have heard the country-western song which hit the radio waves soon after the Jimmy Swaggart scandal. It takes little imagination to understand the tongue-in-cheek lyrics as coming from the wife of a disgraced television evangelist:

> God may forgive you, but I won't;
> Yes, Jesus loves you, but I don't.
>
> You say you're born again, well so am I;
> They don't have to live with you, neither do I.
>
> God may forgive you, but I won't,
> I won't even try.

The derisive sentiment, belted out to the accompaniment of a rhythm section and backup guitars, raises all the serious questions which revolve around the spectacle of a fallen spiritual leader. Does God forgive him? If so, should we? Even if we forgive him, do we still have to "live" with him? If we find it difficult either to forgive him or to live with him, do we nevertheless have a Christian obligation to try?

The rejoicing of the world when we fall on our faces is to be expected. They gloat, they strut, they tell us, "We told you so!" David knew the scorn of his enemies, and he answered with lyrics of his own:

How long, O Lord? Will you forget me
    me forever?
How long will you hide your face
    from me?
How long must I wrestle with my thoughts
    and every day have sorrow in my heart?
How long will my enemy triumph over me?

Look on me and answer, O Lord my God.
    Give light to my eyes, or I will sleep
    in death;
My enemy will say, "I have overcome him,"
    and my foes will rejoice when I fall.

But I trust in your unfailing love;
    my heart rejoices in your salvation.
I will sing to the Lord,
    for he has been good to me.
                —Psalm 13

A contrite heart like David's makes us want to forgive, forget, and forbear in any way we can, as soon as we can. Such a broken spirit invites conciliation and restoration. But not all who fall evoke the same reaction from us. In prophesying against Nineveh, the prophet Nahum expressed the kind of feelings we are likely to have about the hypocrite who has fallen because of his own insensitivity to others:

Nothing can heal your wound;
    your injury is fatal.
Everyone who hears the news about you
    claps his hands at your fall,
for who has not felt
    your endless cruelty?
                —Nahum 3:19

And who can miss the outrage directed at the arrogance of Babylon, through the words of Jeremiah?

"See, I am against you, O arrogant one,"
   declares the Lord, the Lord Almighty,
"for your day has come,
      the time for you to be punished.
The arrogant one will stumble and
      fall and no one will help her up;
I will kindle a fire in her towns that
      will consume all who are around her."
                              —Jeremiah 50:31,32

Words spoken about an entire nation seem equally appropriate for fallen spiritual leaders whose arrogance has preceded them. Forgiveness and restoration are longer in coming when one encounters a haughty heart.

Even so, the writer of Proverbs warns against our hoping for another person's downfall, and rebukes our rejoicing at the failings of our enemies:

Do not lie in wait like an outlaw against a
      righteous man's house,
   do not raid his dwelling place;
for though a righteous man falls seven
      times, he rises again,
   but the wicked are brought down by
      calamity.

Do not gloat when your enemy falls;
   when he stumbles, do not let your
      heart rejoice,
or the Lord will see and disapprove
   and turn his wrath away from him.
                              —Proverbs 24:15-18

Have we rejoiced when those with whom we disagree on doctrinal issues have experienced moral catastrophe? Have their personal spiritual falls given us a smug sense of justification for our own position, as if there were some automatic connection between their doctrine and their sin? Do we make the same inference when some-one who happens to agree with us doctrinally also falls?

Have we rejoiced over the misfortune of those whose particular ministry or preaching style offends us? Have their personal spiritual falls allowed us to say to our-selves that we were right all along? Were we sitting around eagerly awaiting the inevitable? In addition to finding a way to forgive *them*, we may need to ask for-giveness for *our own* attitudes.

When *anyone* who is seen by the world as a Christian leader falls into disgrace, we *all* fall into disgrace. Worse yet, the name of Christ is tarnished. There is simply no reason for rejoicing at another person's fall, even if we happen not to like him personally or what we think he represents.

But what of the spiritual leaders who have led us with sensitivity and humility, yet have slipped and fallen victim to sin? Do we write them off? Do we say, "Sorry, but you're not in the picture anymore. You've embar-rassed us too much to be worthy of our continued friendship. And don't even think about ever stepping into a leadership role again!"

Solomon must have heard lines like those from a lot of good brothers and sisters when he fell off his pedestal and broke their admiring hearts. Everyone loves a hero, but nobody wants to associate with a hero who lets himself become human. You can almost see Solomon, older and even wiser by experience, sitting alone on the hillside overlooking Jerusalem, reflecting on how his fair-weather friends had abandoned him in his hour of need. With their self-righteous rebuffs still raging in his memory, he slowly reaches for a writing tablet and shares this wisdom for generations to come: "If one falls down, his friend can help him up. But pity the man who falls and has no one to help him up!" (Ecclesiastes 4:10).

I love knowing that I am a "child" of God. It makes me feel secure in the knowledge that, even if everyone else abandons me, I have a loving Father who cares. When I trip and stumble, he picks me up, dusts me off, and points me once again in the right direction. King David must have felt the same way. In fact, David felt as if, no matter how shocking his conduct had been, in God's eyes it was not a "fall" but only a "stumble."

> The Lord delights in the way of the man
>   whose steps he has made firm;
> though he stumble, he will not fall,
>   for the Lord upholds him with his
>   hand.
>   —Psalm 37:23,24

Through the prophet Jeremiah, God expressed more confidence in us than we normally have in ourselves or in other people: "When men fall down, do they not get up? When a man turns away, does he not return" (Jeremiah 8:4)?

Restoration is God's way. He brings us back when we have fallen away. When Israel yielded to the temptation of idolatry, God rescued the nation from the captivity of its sin and circled his forgiving arms around his people, as he had done time and time again. And if God lifts his people from the depths of disgrace, how could we do less?

Beyond Forgiveness, A Harder Question

For most of us, forgiveness of another person is always a possibility. In fact, given enough time, forgiveness is usually an eventuality. But *forgetting* is hardly ever possible. No one will easily forget the recent scandals which have rocked the Christian community. Nor will we ever forget the disgrace attached to Gary Hart, Richard Nixon, or, for that matter, Abraham, Moses, David, or Peter. We will always remember.

Yet isn't it interesting *how* we tend to remember Abraham, Moses, David, and Peter? We rarely think of them as the sinners they were. We think of them as great men of God. Unfortunately, history probably will not be as kind to Hart and Nixon. But why the distinction? Why should theirs be a different case?

In some ways we are comparing apples and oranges, since Hart and Nixon do not fall naturally into the category of "men of God." They were not called to be leaders of God's people. But if we dig deeper, we will see more significant differences than the obvious ones. Without presuming to know his spiritual relationship with God, did you ever get the sense that Gary Hart was penitent? Of course, even a penitent Gary Hart likely would have been forced out of presidential contention. But certainly without repentance his political doom was sealed.

Richard Nixon is an even better example. Following the Watergate scandal and his fall from the presidency, Nixon was officially pardoned of all illegal activity while in office. But forgiveness from a broken nation was slow in coming. I keep thinking how different it might have been if Nixon had ever once genuinely confessed his wrongdoing. There were expressions of regret, but never a truly penitent confession. If presidential pride had led to his fall, perhaps the same pride prevented true repentance as well.

The effectual working of a penitent heart, seen in Watergate participant Chuck Colson, for example, stands in stark contrast. In his case, the penitentiary in which he was confined actually lived up to its name. Penitence brought him back into national respect and, even more important, into a new relationship with God.

All of this leads one to believe that we are able not only to forgive but also to forget, when we perceive true repentance and sincere confession on the part of a fallen leader. It's not that we forget the sin; rather, we forget to think of the sinner *as* a sinner. Where there is true repentance and sincere confession, a kind of "godly amnesia" allows us to give the sinner a fresh start, with no strings attached. The record of his sin is expunged, as if it never existed. Sure, in the back of our minds we remember there is a file on him somewhere, but for the life of us we can't remember what it contained.

But this only compels a further question: How can we ever know whether a person's repentance is genuine? Is the fallen leader confessing because he is filled with remorse, or simply because he got caught? Is confession a true picture of one's heart, or is it merely a photo opportunity?

Some might ask, "If spiritual leaders were really repentant, why does it take public disclosure of their sin to prompt a dramatic confession?" What seems to be a reasonable question overlooks the possibility that there may have been private repentance and confession to God while the sin was still private. The public confession may only have been made necessary by public awareness of the sin. This is, in fact, the exact case of one prominent spiritual leader whose unfaithfulness to his wife had already been disclosed to her and dealt with privately before word of the affair became public.

We cannot assume, therefore, that public confessions are simply salvage efforts by calculating sinners desperate to minimize the damage and maintain their positions of leadership. On the other hand, that possibility always remains. So how are we to know the difference?

One clue may be the quickness with which a confession of sin is forthcoming. Confessions which come only after repeated denials should certainly be suspect. If the tears begin to roll down the cheek only after incriminating evidence reaches insurmountable heights, one has to wonder about the genuineness of a dramatic confession.

Another clue to true repentance may be the sinner's humility in dropping out of his leadership role. If there is insistence on maintaining one's position despite obvious scandal and disgrace, undoubtedly there are still heart problems to be dealt with. What conscientious spiritual leader could allow himself to be a continuing stumbling block on the path to Christ? What sensitive man of God would even have the moral fortitude to face so quickly the many people he has disappointed?

We will not always have the kind of certainty we would like regarding the genuineness of one's repentance. But the best clues will always come from the attitude of the fallen leader himself. John the Baptist set a pretty high standard for those wanting reconciliation with God. "Produce fruit in keeping with repentance," he insisted.

How about several years spent quietly on the mission field? How about sharing the suffering of alienation with those who suffer daily on the streets and in the ghettos? How about bowing before God in daily prayer and devotion in some quiet place away from the limelight for a long enough time to get calluses on the knees? What else could repentance mean for those who have stood so tall and fallen so far?

To Err Is Human; To Restore Is Too Much to Ask

Suppose we are convinced of the genuineness of one's repentance. Does this mean that restoration is in order? Yes. You mean it's that simple? Yes. But surely it depends on the circumstances? No. Are you telling us that restoration, in every case, *must* follow true repentance? Absolutely!

We must abandon forever the notion that fallen spiritual leaders are irredeemable and expendable. That is as unscriptural a notion as automatically divorcing a spouse who has been unfaithful. If, on the day of judgment, God were to treat us like most fallen spiritual leaders are treated, all of us "forgiven" sinners would end up in hell! Forgiveness means acceptance. It does not mean ostracism and divorce.

I particularly like the assessment of our typical reaction to David's situation, as told by management consultant Robert Dingman:

> Sometimes I wonder how King David would have fared in a church-related job interview. Before Bathsheba caught his attention, he would have delighted the search committee. But after that tragic fall, the search committee would have clearly labeled him "damaged goods."

Using David as his example, Dingman leaves us with still another important insight into the acceptance of fallen spiritual leaders:

> I contend that David was a much better candidate *after* Bathsheba, as was Peter after his denials of Christ. People who have experienced the penalties of error have often received an inoculation that gives a future immunity.

If not future immunity, at least greater insight, compassion, and resolution to overcome.

The question can never be "Shall we restore the penitent fallen spiritual leader?" Otherwise we have not understood forgiveness. Forgiveness *implies* healing and restoration. There are only two questions we are permitted to ask: "When?" and "How?"

How Soon the Restoration?

As for "When," it is doubtful whether arbitrary periods of rehabilitation are realistic. Prespecified periods of probation, such as one-year or two-year absences from the pulpit, are more likely to resemble criminal sentences than to actually achieve the kind of healing that precedes restoration. When we talk of rehabilitation for the offender, we sometimes forget that healing must take place on the other side of the fence as well. Until the church has come to terms with the trust that has been broken by its leader, restoration cannot be effective.

Leadership, like money, is made the old-fashioned way—you *earn* it. Spiritual leadership is never bestowed or removed arbitrarily; it is bound up with relationship. A wife's submission to her husband is not an abstract duty tied to her wedding ring; it is based on the husband's own duty of spiritual leadership which God has called him to exercise on behalf of the family. Likewise, a congregation's responsibility to submit to its leaders' spiritual guidance grows out of a relationship of trust and respect. And no clock or calendar can dictate the formation, termination, or restoration of such a relationship.

In determining when to restore, we must take into consideration not only the leader's relationship with the church, but also his standing with those outside the church. If he is still held in disrepute from those on the outside, does he not continue to be unfit for spiritual leadership despite the acceptance of his Christian brothers and sisters? If to *become* a spiritual leader he must have had a good reputation with outsiders (1 Timothy 3:7), must he not also have a good reputation before he can be *restored* as a spiritual leader?

The withholding of a position of recognized leadership under those circumstances is not a commentary on one's personal acceptability in the eyes of God or the church. Nor does failure to reinstate him officially prevent him from going about informally doing the work of a spiritual leader. But giving him a badge of approval when the world is looking on with scorn can only be a stumbling block to their potential faith in a God who calls us to uncompromising holiness.

How long, then, before a fallen spiritual leader should be restored? As long as it takes. And not a minute before.

Nor, for wrong reasons, a minute too late.

In What Way the Restoration?

As for the "How," we have finally arrived at the point where we can say, "It depends upon the circumstances." Perhaps there is much we can learn from the manner in which Jesus restored Peter. He allowed Peter to restore himself in the same way that he had disgraced himself— by acknowledging his commitment to Jesus, where before Peter had denied him. Remember that scene on the shore of the Sea of Tiberias after Jesus' resurrection? Not once, but three times, Jesus asked Peter if he loved him. And each time Peter affirmed that he did. Reading the account of Peter's reinstatement, you get the feeling that, had Peter denied Jesus 20 times, Jesus likewise would have put to Peter the question of his loyalty 20 times.

The principle of restoration which may be suggested by that incident is the requirement of proven faithfulness in the area of one's weakness. It is something akin to making the punishment fit the crime. We must be careful, of course, not to play favorites among sins, simply because the fallen leader's sin was not *our* sin. It is all too easy to see our own sin as merely a "weakness" and other people's sins as great moral outrages. Our self-righteousness in making such distinctions may itself be the greater sin.

Yet another critical question needs to be asked. In restoring a renowned spiritual leader, should we require *more* of him because he has caused more widespread disgrace to the church, or *less* of him because he has done so much good up to the point of his fall? I don't presume to know the answer, but I might suggest at least this: Surely a person who has contributed greatly to the spiritual growth of others is entitled to more consideration than others who have done very little in the work of the Lord.

The sad irony is that, on the strength of one sin, we often forget all the good that a person has done. Our sense of betrayal wants to cancel the credits one has built up over many years of faithful service. It is sort of an "all-or-nothing" situation, which clearly cannot be right.

Naturally, it is also possible that we could lean over backward *too* far on behalf of a beloved fallen leader. One way to check that tendency is to ask whether we would treat another brother or sister in the Lord—who has been equally fruitful in the Lord's work, but never in a position of prominence—with equally sympathetic consideration. Good credit should not come with prominence alone.

Before we make any crucial decision about a fallen leader, it might be well if we took time to "walk a mile in his moccasins." Would we think our decision to be fair if we were in *his* shoes? Certainly such a self-serving conclusion would not always be the bottom line, but it should be part of our deliberations.

Once again, the perception of those who are outside the church may also be a vital consideration. On one hand, we should do what is right, regardless of what the whole world might think. Their judgment is not spiritually based. On the other hand, more than one scripture points to the need for maintaining credibility with those who are on the outside looking in. Our decision could be so hypocritically protective that it is received with howls of derision.

Finally, there is yet one more question we must consider: Must we assume in every case that restoration always means *exact* restoration? Are we left with the choice of either restoring the leader to the same position which he formerly held or discarding him altogether? Too often, as part of our "all-or-nothing" approach, we ignore alternative possibilities.

If one is to be banned from the pulpit, for example, is there no teaching role he can fill? If, for a time, one is unsuitable as a teacher, might he not become a counselor to others, who are his fellow sinners? If public interaction seems inadvisable, is there something behind the scenes to which he could contribute? The leader's sin is disgrace enough. We don't need to compound the disgrace by throwing away sorely needed skills or, worse yet, a precious soul.

The More Difficult Task

I've just been doing some remodeling in my little English cottage. Tearing out the wall between the match-box-size living and dining rooms seemed to be the answer to my need for customary American spaciousness. Up the road I noticed some men restoring a lovely old house in the village. The stonework they were doing was beautiful. You could tell they really knew their business. So I asked them whether in their spare time they might tear out my wall. They said they would be happy to do it.

Within a couple of days, Roy and Gilbert knocked on the door, ready to go to work. When they discovered a brick wall, instead of the studded wall they expected, they were undaunted. Wielding sledgehammers and cranes, they mounted a furious attack on the enemy. Dust flew, bricks crumbled, and wallboard fell in defeated heaps onto the floor. Within a couple of hours I could stand in the little dining room and look right at the stone fireplace in the living room. I was thrilled!

But phase two of the operation has been a different story. It has been three weeks now since the great day of destruction, and the place still isn't put back together. Every other day or so Roy and Gilbert show up to do "bits and bobs," as the British say. A little hammering here, a little plastering there. The fury of destruction has been replaced with the now-standard farewell: "We'll be back in the next day or two."

I've grown to like Roy and Gilbert, both of whom are weathered construction workers nearing retirement age. They couldn't be more well-meaning or helpful. Unfortunately, I've discovered that their carpentry is not quite up to the standards of their masonry. Corners are not exactly squared, and a gap here or there doesn't seem to bother them quite as much as it does me. But I'm trying not to fuss too much about it. The price is certainly right, and I've acquired two new friends.

It occurs to me that my little construction job demonstrates quite pointedly how we usually go about the work of restoration. Most of us are very good at tearing down, but awfully slow and negligent in building up again. At the first sign of sin in a spiritual leader, we take up our sledgehammers and attack with a vengeance. The more dust and rubble the better. Just get rid of him, as quickly as possible. But once the damage is done, we can't seem to get on with the task of restoration. We hammer a bit here and patch a bit there, but we don't always cut square corners, and there are tremendous gaps in what we do on our fallen leader's behalf.

Sometimes we just try to whitewash the whole matter, leaving glaring flaws to take care of themselves. Sometimes we employ pieces of advice and counsel that simply do not fit. We may be sincere and well-meaning, but the job just isn't done right. It hardly matters that we are very good at accomplishing other spiritual tasks. When it comes to the restoration of fallen spiritual leaders, most of us are simply out of our territory.

Lord, make us fit for the task we hope never to do. Help us to rebuke where necessary and to restore where possible—ever looking to our own sin as a reminder that we are all unworthy servants. When spiritual leaders fall, let us hear again the words of Paul to the Colossians (3:12-14):

> Therefore, as God's chosen people, holy and dearly loved, clothe yourselves with compassion, kindness, humility, gentleness and patience. Bear with each other and forgive whatever grievances you may have against one another. Forgive as the Lord forgave you. And over all these virtues put on love, which binds them all together in perfect unity.

Looking Within

- Do you take great delight in the fact that someone you know, or know of, has fallen spiritually? Have you considered the impact of his fall on the Christian community, or on your own credibility, or—worse yet—on the work of God?
- Is there someone you need to forgive? Can you think of a better time than now?
- Is there something you need to forget so that you can go on with your life and be productive for the Lord? What is standing in your way?
- Do you have sin in your life that you will confess and turn away from only if you happen to get caught? Does it mean nothing that God is already grieving about it?
- If you have forgiven someone lately, have you gone the extra mile to make sure his restoration is complete? To see if there is some way you can be a strength to him?

12

Who Is Equal to Such a Task?

Preventing the Problems

Sandwiched between my experience as a criminal prosecutor and my career as a law professor was a brief but enlightening professional detour. I spent a year in Portland, Oregon, as Director of Admission and Professional Conduct for the Oregon State Bar, wearing essentially two administrative hats. Under the first hat I was in charge of administering the bar examination to applicants for admission to the bar. It was sweet revenge for having had to experience that baptism of fire for myself just three years earlier.

Under the second (and much larger) hat I was in charge of handling complaints submitted to the bar office against Oregon attorneys. I must say that the number of complaints we received was overwhelming to an idealistic young attorney only three years out of law school. I still had the idea that lawyers were getting a bad rap when maligned as ambulance chasers, thieves, and pettifoggers. Unfortunately, my year at the Oregon State Bar was a disillusioning experience. In retrospect, I can guarantee you that spiritual leaders are not the only ones who fall.

Within a six-month period, complaints were received against fully one-fourth of all actively practicing Oregon attorneys! What I found most disturbing was the inadequacy of the disciplinary process to move quickly to suspend or disbar those few attorneys who were serious miscreants. It took an average of three years for a guilty attorney to lose his license to practice! What's more, many less-blatant yet obvious violations were completely white-washed. In order to be kicked out of the bar, an attorney practically had to murder someone. As you can see, the church has no exclusive claim to problems regarding discipline and restoration.

More intriguing than all of this, I discovered that attorneys are rarely the perpetrators of specific viola-tions of the Rules of Professional Conduct. Few attor-neys knowingly and intentionally lie, cheat, or steal. Where attorneys get themselves into trouble are the little things which they could easily avoid: failure to commu-nicate sufficiently with their clients, delay in handling cases, or not fully explaining their fees. As much as anything, complaints arise out of relationship problems.

At one point in my brief tenure at the bar, I tried to analyze why it was that so many complaints were being lodged for conduct which didn't come close to violating the code. Several patterns emerged. First was a kind of professional arrogance among lawyers. *We* are attorneys; *they* are just clients. *We* are professionals; *they* are just ordinary laymen. *We* have a knowledge of the law; *they*, of course, know nothing.

Second was a technocratic approach to lawyering. To the lawyer, the client looks like an interesting legal issue, or an $8^1/_2$ x 14 manila file folder containing just another law school hypothetical to analyze and solve. As legal technicians, lawyers know the law; but as legal coun-selors, they can't seem to relate the law to the personal needs of the client.

Still another pattern emerged, most often among criminal lawyers. Many seemed to have a proclivity for lowering themselves to their clients' level. It is not unlike what happens to some police officers who spend their life rubbing elbows with what they come to consider human rubbish. After awhile the officers begin to talk like they talk, think like they think, and act like they act.

Finally, another pattern I discovered—what might be called the "pressure-cooker syndrome"—probably stems from a common personality trait among lawyers, who tend to be workaholics. Among the many problems attaching to workaholics are stress, fatigue, and deterioration of personal relationships. In the case of lawyers, you see the destructiveness in a higher-than-average divorce rate on the home front and mistreatment of clients in the office. Lawyers often take on more cases than they can handle, and find themselves shortchanging their clients. In a system that already thrives on delay, the overburdened lawyer finds himself in a morass of inaction. Again, the client is the loser.

All in all, if the legal profession often exceeds its public image through conscientious service to most of its clients, it also often falls far short of its own lofty ideals.

How God's Men of Law Rate

I have a feeling that we might get very similar results if there were a central organization to receive complaints against spiritual leaders. In his second letter to the Christians at Corinth, Paul writes as if he were experienced as a Director of Professional Conduct for such an organization. Almost the entire letter is a textbook for proper leadership conduct. If in this book we have concentrated on the problems of fallen spiritual leaders, Paul's letter charts a path to prevention.

We have already pointed out that, like lawyers, spiritual leaders face the great temptation of professional arrogance. It is bolstered by education, degrees, titles, special regalia, and positions of honor and respect within the community. It is easy for all of us to think more highly of ourselves than we ought. Therefore, Paul's advice is that we remind ourselves constantly that our confidence is "through Christ before God. Not that we are competent in ourselves to claim anything for ourselves, but our competence comes from God" (2 Corinthians 3:4,5).

What this means, of course, is that we will be ever more cautious about elevating ourselves in the cause of Christ, "for we do not preach ourselves, but Jesus Christ as Lord, and ourselves as your servants for Jesus' sake" (2 Corinthians 4:5). The relationship between humility and servanthood ensures that, with humility, we never lose sight of whom we serve.

Like lawyers, we get into trouble when we separate ourselves from those we serve. It happens when those in the "clergy" look upon those in the "laity" as second-class, when we act paternalistically in their behalf as if they were spiritually inferior. Knowing that lofty pedestals inevitably lead to spiritual falls, Paul admonishes us to stay close to Christ, the ultimate Servant-Leader who never fell.

Technocrats and Freewheelers

Law, whether God's law or man's law, has a nasty habit of grabbing the spotlight, as if it were *the law itself* that is important rather than what the law is supposed to accomplish. Undoubtedly that is why Jesus reminded us to give attention to "the weightier matters of the law." We can obey the law in every detail yet miss altogether what it is designed to bring about in our lives.

It is equally true of both God's law and man's law that those who are entrusted with administering and teaching the law can also distort their focus. We saw earlier where legal technocrats are very good at *knowing* the law but not always so good at sensitively *using* the law. Among spiritual leaders there may also be technocrats, whose knowledge of God's laws may actually be a stumbling block for themselves.

For example, the biblical scholar who has devoted his

life to exploring every jot and tittle of the law may know the Book backward and forward but have little appreciation for its message. He may know the Book without knowing the God of the Book. He may have academic information but not personal relation. If so, such a spiritual leader is on a collision course with disaster when temptation comes his way. His M.Div. degree will prove of little value in a deadly struggle with sin.

At the other extreme is the spiritual leader who has neither formal academic biblical training nor adequate knowledge of the Scriptures from personal study. He may think he has a dynamic relationship with God, but he is not securely grounded in sound doctrine through the Word. Of such Paul said, "They want to be teachers of the law, but they do not know what they are talking about or what they so confidently affirm" (1 Timothy 1:7). When temptation comes to such a spiritual leader, his shooting from the hip, armed only with moral instinct, is likely to get himself shot in the foot.

Fortunately, most spiritual leaders are in neither extreme category. Unfortunately, however, most spiritual leaders have a bit of both in them. The natural tendencies are to assume immunity from spiritual failure simply because one has more knowledge of the Scriptures than other people, and, alternately, to assume that one can "wing it" simply because he is a "man of God."

The danger in either approach is self-reliance, based on one's own understanding or personal spirituality, rather than on the strength which comes from God. In law we have an adage which says, "A lawyer who represents himself has a fool for a client." The adage obviously has an interesting application when applied to spiritual leaders who place their defense against sin in their own fallible hands.

If you ever wanted to find a group of people who

experience the rush of power in their veins, it is lawyers. With but flimsy pieces of paper they can make a defendant's blood run cold. They can order people to jump, and they have to jump. They can stop buildings from being built, take children away from parents, and decide whether the plug will be pulled in the intensive-care unit. Yet spiritual leaders have even more potential for moving in people's lives—even affecting eternal destinies! Is it any wonder, then, that Paul reminds us: "But we have this treasure in jars of clay to show that this all-surpassing power is from God and not from us" (2 Corinthians 4:7).

We are only conduits, not the source. We are vessels, not the contents. We are messengers, not the message. And what power we might demonstrate in support of the message must always be credited to him from whom all power proceeds. If we fail to give God the credit, we will deceive even ourselves about how powerful we are. And then when temptation comes, chances are we will overestimate our power to resist it.

Following the Followers

I mentioned criminal lawyers and their risk of reflecting the standards of those with whom they associate. Bill D. Hallsted, minister of the Church of Christ in Truman, Minnesota, suggests that spiritual leaders can find themselves caught up in what he calls "Sin saturation."

> Week after week a torrent of sins needing forgiveness flows past our awareness until we may begin to lose sense of the awfulness of sin. We who ought to hate sin more than anyone because we so constantly see its devastating effect can become the most blase toward it.
>
> We've seen so many gross sins that when we are then tempted, it may seem such a minor

thing if we, too, should sin: *All that forgiveness will surely cover me, won't it? (Leadership,* Winter 1988, p. 19).

When sinning spiritual leaders begin to look good by comparison with those who confess "even greater" sins, watch out! The spiritual leader who allows himself to think comparatively is headed for sure defeat. If our ministry is to the spiritually dead, we must resolve all the more to be spiritually alive, "for we who are alive are always being given over to death for Jesus' sake, so that his life may be revealed in our mortal body" (2 Corinthians 4:11).

As spiritual leaders for other people who are caught up in sin, our sympathy and even our empathy is always in order—but never our company.

Closer from a Distance

Hallsted also points to another problem that is common to both lawyers and spiritual leaders, if perhaps for different reasons. While I wouldn't characterize most spiritual leaders I know as workaholics, as I would most lawyers, the fact is that their ministry often fatigues them mentally, emotionally, and spiritually. Hallsted points to what he calls "job overload."

It seems close to blasphemy to say we need time away from the things of God. Maybe that's why so many are unwilling to say it, let alone secure it.

Everyone else needs a break from thinking about jobs and the demands of work. Since our "job" surrounds us with the things of God, our minds need a similar rest. It's only natural.

Yet so much do our minds need a hiatus from constant religious exposure that we can find ourselves vulnerable to amusement far removed from the things of God, and our society offers limitless opportunities for such escape. They're as close as the television knob, the magazine rack, or the bookstore. And they sully the hands of God's workers.

Perhaps owing to his legal training, and to what seems to be a workaholic personality trait—not to mention the built-in burdens of spiritual leadership—the apostle Paul appears to have suffered much from stress and fatigue. Indeed, he talks about being "hard pressed on every side, but not crushed; perplexed, but not in despair; persecuted, but not abandoned; struck down, but not destroyed" (2 Corinthians 4:8,9). With all that pressure, what kept him from caving in? Reading between the lines, one gets the feeling his ability to cope came from a life-balancing *perspective*.

> Therefore we do not lose heart. Though outwardly we are wasting away, yet inwardly we are being renewed day by day. For our light and momentary troubles are achieving for us an eternal glory that far outweighs them all. So we fix our eyes not on what is seen, but on what is unseen. For what is seen is temporary, but what is unseen is eternal (2 Corinthians 4:16-18).

Yet, as Bill Hallsted has suggested, perspective must be maintained by actual physical breaks from the work of our high calling. It is the God-given principle of sabbatical rest, relaxation, and renewal.

Jess Moody suggests we may need to hit more golf balls—just to get rid of the frustration we feel. Hit one for the deacon who is all over your back for forgetting to make the announcement he requested. Hit one for the elder who thinks you haven't been denouncing his favorite target with sufficient force or regularity. Indeed, for the rest of us, hit one for the preacher who week after week preaches Pablum pieties that drive us up a wall with their sublime emptiness.

The principle of sabbatical rest means time away from one's congregation—not in a retreat with other spiritual leaders, but away altogether. And not only for further academic pursuit, but for a time of quiet reflection. A time to see God's handiwork in nature. A time to renew relationship with the family. Without such breaks, one often loses even the perspective to which Paul referred.

I am impressed with how many times Jesus went off to a quiet place by himself—to pray, to meditate on the challenges ahead, perhaps to double-check his priorities, and simply to be at peace with his Father, far from the madding crowd. If the Son of God felt a need for personal spiritual retreats in his life, why should we think we could give a lifetime of spiritual service at nonstop, breakneck pace?

Local congregations need to recognize how crucial sabbatical breaks are for their leaders. We might even be happily surprised by fresh insight and perspective wafting down from the pulpit. Christian colleges need to encourage sabbaticals, not only for research and writing, but for spiritual refreshment. And college administrators themselves, on whose shoulders rest the responsibility of maintaining Christian commitment amid the pressures of a secular world, should periodically step away from their "irreplaceable roles" to nurture and give direction to their personal commitments to God.

The Problem of Rootlessness

Other lifestyle changes may also be suggested for the

pressure-wearied person of God. At a recent small-group session for ministers, a well-known spiritual leader whose fall from grace has been widely publicized gave this advice: "Don't get too far from your moorings. If you do a lot of traveling, get off the road! Stay home with those you love. Let them nurture you and keep you on an even keel." Certainly his advice leads to safety, security, and serenity.

How do spiritual leaders end up in the ditch? Sometimes they are on the road so much that they end up making wrong turns.

The basic problem here is one of rootlessness—getting too far away from one's roots, one's support system. Rootlessness is most often experienced by spiritual leaders who are constantly in demand, always on the go. The roots of family, office, and one's home church are replaced by other roots—airplanes, airports, endless hotel rooms, and an untold number of restaurants along the "fast lane" of life.

The new roots not only fail to nourish but they in fact pull one away from the direction of his own values and his message to others. They pull one away from both professional and personal accountability.

And if anyone is particularly affected by rootlessness, it is the young person on the way up. The problem of people undertaking spiritual leadership at a young age is exacerbated in that their roots are not as well-developed in their lives. When everything else in your life is in swift transition, it is all too easy for values to become victims of that transition.

As suggested earlier, the best answer is for the spiritual leader to renegotiate with himself, and with his wife and family, to stay closer to his real roots: to stay home more often, to get involved in ministries in closer proximity, and to commit time to those among whom he serves nearby.

Money, Money—Always the Problem

How often the fall of spiritual leaders has been caused by money—the love of it, the abuse of it, the *appearance* of abuse of it! Like some lawyers, we are in positions of trust which often lead to our handling of other people's money. Like some lawyers, some spiritual leaders simply cannot resist the temptation to misuse those funds. Judas was but the first in a long line of men of God dipping into the till.

But of course there is more than one way to dip into the till. Money need not be stolen outright; it may simply be used for purposes never intended. It may come in the form of exorbitant fees (for lawyers) or exorbitant salaries or unreported fringe benefits (for spiritual leaders). It can even come in the misplacement of priorities, such as putting church buildings above benevolence and evangelism.

But we have a higher calling: "Unlike so many, we do not peddle the word of God for profit. On the contrary, in Christ we speak before God with sincerity, like men sent from God" (2 Corinthians 2:17). As we approach others to lead them to Christ, we must say in our hearts, "I will not be a burden to you, because what I want is not your possessions but you" (2 Corinthians 12:14). Armed with that attitude, if ever we were brought up on charges, God forbid, we could say with confidence, "We have wronged no one, we have corrupted no one, we have exploited no one" (2 Corinthians 7:2).

Naturally, the best defense is a good offense. The best way to avoid being "brought up on charges" is to avoid "the very appearance of evil." I cannot help but wonder if there is more than coincidence to the fact that, in a letter almost exclusively devoted to the responsibilities of spiritual leaders, Paul writes to the Corinthians about taking up a collection for their fellow Christians in Judea. Certainly he was addressing a particular need at a particular time. But it is at least fortuitous that his discussion of the collection focuses in on one of the most serious problems facing spiritual leaders—the handling of church money.

Look with what caution and detail Paul arranges for the conveyance of their love gift. He sent not only Titus but two other highly respected brothers in order to make sure that the funds got where they were supposed to go, with no questions raised.

> For Titus not only welcomed our appeal, but he is coming to you with much enthusiasm and on his own initiative. And we are sending along with him the brother who is praised by all the churches for his service to the gospel. What is more, he was chosen by the churches to accompany us as we carry the offering, which we administer in order to honor the Lord himself and to show our eagerness to help. We want to avoid any criticism of the way we administer this liberal gift. For we are taking pains to do what is right, not only in the eyes of the Lord but also in the eyes of men.
>
> In addition, we are sending with them our brother who has often proved to us in many ways that he is zealous, and now even more so because of his great confidence in you. As for Titus, he is my partner and fellow worker among you; as for our brothers, they are representatives of the churches and an honor to Christ (2 Corinthians 8:17-23).

Such precautions are not a sign of distrust for those who might be in charge of church contributions, any more than the requirement that lawyers keep their personal account and client funds separate. It is simply a way to avoid having anyone face unnecessary temptation, and to provide verification in the event that anyone should call into question the handling of funds.

If this suggested procedure for being open and above-board is important in the church itself, it is even more important in parachurch organizations. Already we have seen fiscal disaster and scandal where open accountability did not exist.

Recently the National Religious Broadcasters approved a stringent code of ethics for the electronic church, and set up its Ethics and Financial Integrity Commission to police a kind of "Good Housekeeping Seal of Approval" for religious broadcasters. Another watchdog organization, the Evangelical Council for Financial Accountability, mandates financial reporting and sets other protective guidelines for its 405 members (with financial resources totaling 1.75 billion dollars).

Unfortunately, some of this voluntary accountability failed recently when a major ministry supplied misleading records to organization auditors. One who is a Christian hardly need be reminded, but, knowing that there are always some who live in the shadowy wasteland of veiled truth, Paul does indeed remind us of who we are and how we are to behave in the house of God. "We have renounced secret and shameful ways," he writes; "we do not use deception, nor do we distort the word of God."

I am not disposed to unnecessarily naming names, but I am appalled at the continuing refusal of some major ministries to fully disclose their financial income and expenditures, even in the light of recent scandal. But maybe that is the very problem: Perhaps they are scurrying about putting their house in order. We can only hope that this is the correct interpretation. It is all too easy for millions of dollars in donations to give new meaning to the phrase "profits without honor"!

Have you ever considered the context of that well-known reference to the love of money being the root of all kinds of evil? It comes in Paul's first letter to Timothy, immediately on the heels of a warning about false teachers, "who think that godliness is a means to financial gain" (1 Timothy 6:3-10). It is hard to think that anyone would wish to profit from the gospel, but there is just too much proof of its happening. We might well take Paul's advice to Timothy as our own: "But you, man of God, flee from all this" (1 Timothy 6:11).

A Higher Calling

The time has come for asking the bottom-line question: When push comes to shove, what is our motivation for spiritual leadership? If not financial gain, power, prestige, or popularity, what is the force that drives us? For Paul, the answer was found in a higher calling: "For we are to God the aroma of Christ among those who are being saved and those who are perishing" (2 Corinthians 2:15). "It is written: 'I believed; therefore I have spoken.' With that same spirit of faith we also believe and therefore speak" (4:13). "Since, then, we know what it is to fear the Lord, we try to persuade men" (5:11). "For Christ's love compels us" (5:14). "We are therefore Christ's ambassadors, as though God were making his appeal through us" (5:20).

With such a lofty motivation for our ministry, how could we dare dishonor ourselves in Christ's service? Paul was well aware of spiritual falls among spiritual leaders. He knew how accusations and charges can come so easily to one's doorstep, whether warranted or unwarranted. But if he were going to suffer, it would be as a spiritual leader whose suffering came from good, not evil.

We put no stumbling block in anyone's path,
so that our ministry will not be discredited.

> Rather, as servants of God we commend our-
> selves in every way; in great endurance; in
> troubles, hardships and distresses; in beat-
> ings, imprisonments and riots; in hard work,
> sleepless nights and hunger; in purity, under-
> standing, patience and kindness; in the Holy
> Spirit and in sincere love; in truthful speech
> and in the power of God; with weapons of
> righteousness in the right hand and in the left;
> through glory and dishonor, bad report and
> good report; genuine, yet regarded as impos-
> tors; known, yet regarded as unknown; dying,
> and yet we live on; beaten, and yet not killed;
> sorrowful, yet always rejoicing; poor, yet mak-
> ing many rich; having nothing, and yet possess-
> ing everything (6:3-10).

If only we could capture the sacrificial spirit of spiritual leadership! Who among us could then fall?

Hit-List Targets

Why do spiritual leaders fall? We could not close the
book without reference to the most obvious reason of all:
Spiritual leaders are targets on the hit list of Satan himself.

All of us are targets, but spiritual leaders are special
targets. After all, they are the ones in the front ranks,
urging others on. If they fall, others will be discouraged.
Leaders are also ripe for the kind of scandal that dis-
credits God in the eyes of the world. They are walking
time bombs for the devil. And how he lurks about,
waiting with delicious anticipation for them to self-
destruct!

Surely that is why James wrote, "Not many of you
should presume to be teachers, my brothers, because
you know that we who teach will be judged more strictly.
We all stumble in many ways" (James 3:1,2).

It happened to one of the best. "Simon, Simon," said Jesus to Peter, "Satan has asked to sift you as wheat" (Luke 22:31). And Peter succumbed—as have we all; as *will* we all. But that is not the end of the story for either Peter or us. "But I have prayed for you, Simon, that your faith may not fail. And when you have turned back, strengthen your brothers" (Luke 22:32).

Satan is out to get us—all of us. Never think otherwise. But God will not let him conquer us. God has work for us to do, whether we are spiritual leaders or whether we are holding up the hands of others who lead. So let the challenge ring again: "And when you have turned back, strengthen your brothers."

"For we are to God the aroma of Christ among those who are being saved and those who are perishing."

"And who is equal to such a task?" Who indeed! God, make us men and women equipped for your sublime service!

Looking Within

- In what do you place your trust for moral security? Is it in your own strength, or your knowledge of the Scriptures, or in God himself?
- Do you regularly take time away from your normal routine and responsibilities for physical rest and relaxation? Or, more important, for spiritual renewal?
- How much of a slave to money have you become? To what extent does the acquiring or the spending of money consume your life?
- What are the roots that are most precious and meaningful to you? If you are often torn away from those roots, is there anything you can do to prevent that from happening?
- Do you see your spiritual life as a constant battle with Satan? If so, who is winning lately?

13

Fallen Ministries, Renewed People

Triumph Out of Tragedy

I recently went back to appear once again on the PTL Show. I continue to be amazed at how comfortable I feel among those with whom I have many differences in doctrine and style. I keep going with bags of skepticism, only to leave with truckloads of appreciation and love. It is always a moving experience for me, reflecting on what has happened to PTL over the past months and years. I walk around the lake in the middle of the Heritage USA complex and contemplate the disaster that has befallen PTL. There, in the reflection of the lake's calm surface, my own personal spiritual disasters are mirrored.

One evening I sat almost alone in the once-bustling cafeteria at the Heritage Grand Hotel. As I looked down Main Street, I saw nothing of the crowds that once flocked to this place. At the weekend the hotel would be much busier, but on this day even a whisper would echo in the empty mall. The sadness was overwhelming. Then, like a burst of light on a dark winter night, the opening words of Lamentations exploded into my mind.

It was as if the ancient writer, touched with the abysmal sorrow of the broken human condition, were describing, not the disgraced fall of Israel's Jerusalem centuries ago, but the terrible fall of PTL. Whatever you may feel about PTL, the poignancy of the writer's lament touches every heart of love.

197

How deserted lies the city,
    once so full of people!
How like a widow is she,
    who once was great among the nations!
She who was queen among the provinces
    has now become a slave....

Among all her lovers
    there is none to comfort her.
All her friends have betrayed her;
    they have become her enemies....

The Lord has brought her grief
    because of her many sins....

All who honored her despise her,
    for they have seen her nakedness....

The enemy laid hands
    on all her treasures;
she saw pagan nations
    enter her sanctuary—
those you had forbidden
    to enter your assembly....

"Look, O Lord, and consider,
    for I am despised."

"Is it nothing to you, all you who pass by?
    Look around and see....

"All my enemies have heard of my distress;
    they rejoice at what you have done."...

How the gold has lost its luster,
    the fine gold become dull!...

Woe to us, for we have sinned!

What words could describe more powerfully the fall of
spiritual leaders? What more memorable an epitaph for
the resulting struggle of a stricken ministry? And what

irony that the idolatry which brought the fall of Jerusalem was but a precursor of the idol-like prominence of Jim and Tammy Bakker!

But when Jerusalem fell, it was not just the spiritual leaders who were destroyed; it was also the thousands of innocents who lay dead in the streets. "All her people groan as they search for bread," says the poet. "Young and old lie together in the dust of the streets; my young men and maidens have fallen by the sword."

As I walk around Heritage USA, everywhere I look I see the innocent victims of one couple's fall. I see dedicated staff members working more than one job at minimum wage to keep heart and home together. I see people who invested life savings, only to believe the cause was lost. I see dreams destroyed, loyalties betrayed, and hearts which are hopeful but hurt. And these are the lucky ones, because there are also many who I don't see at all anymore. Scores who have been laid off since the great fall.

It's not just PTL. It's also the Jimmy Swaggart Ministries, which circled the globe with the message of Christ and with food for the hungry. When one man fell, so did millions of dollars in contributions. When one man sinned, thousands of innocents suffered. No one knows the impact when just one person of God falls!

For all the growing love I have for the good people left behind in the dust of scandal at PTL and elsewhere, I have to suggest that we are still walking the wrong road. Israel fell because she followed misguided leaders into forbidden paths. She fell because she accepted second-best. Are parachurch ministries truly the Lord's will? Have we stopped to ask ourselves whether what we are doing is bound to fail because it is not God's way? Have we invited disaster because we have sought to please God through avenues he never approved? It is indeed a time for introspection:

Let him sit alone in silence,
    for the Lord has laid it on him.
Let him bury his face in the dust—
    there may yet be hope.
Let him offer his cheek to one who would
        strike him,
    and let him be filled with disgrace.

Lord, give us a quiet spirit in your presence. We know that you are in your holy temple as you direct our paths. "Let all the earth keep silence before you."

Lessons for the Learning

But this book is not really about PTL, or disgraced televangelists, or even fallen spiritual leaders within the local church. This book is about you. This book is about me. It is about you and me in our brokenness. It is about the emptiness we feel when we sin, the estrangement we experience in our rebellion, the shame we feel as we stand naked in sin before our God.

PTL is but a picture of brokenness. Fallen televangelists are but a reminder of our own frailty. The Anglican church is but a warning about accepting second-best in our spiritual lives. Sinful men and women of God in the Bible are but monuments to our own vulnerability.

This book is about keeping to the old paths in the work and worship of the church. About walking the high roads of integrity, purity, and right living. About letting God show us the way through his Word. The way that works. The way that satisfies our needs. The way that serves his people.

This book is a call for accountability mixed with compassion. It is a call for forgiveness—of churches, ministries, fallen leaders, and even ourselves. It is a call for mutual love and mutual support, mutual prayers and mutual cares. It is a call for spiritual renewal in the face of disgrace.

Above all, this book is about submission, and consecration, and ongoing repentance—as a way of life! In our discussion together, the question "Why do spiritual leaders fall?" has been answered by a host of good reasons. But, taken together, they can all too easily become excuses for anyone inclined to look for excuses! Attempting to understand the circumstances that can lead us into sin is not meant to let any of us off the hook.

When push comes to shove, spiritual leaders fall into sin for the same reason that everyone else falls: We all yield to temptation. We are not as concerned about sin as we ought to be. We are not as consecrated to holiness as we should be. We are not as committed to God as we could be. With Paul we must say, "I beat my body and make it my slave so that after I have preached to others, I myself will not be disqualified for the prize" (1 Corinthians 9:27).

And if we are tempted to blame everyone and everything but ourselves, we must reaffirm that—whether we stand in the pulpit or sit in the pew—we are totally responsible for our own actions. No one goes to hell in a tour bus. We fall into sin one by one, each on our own.

Far from dredging up excuses or blaming anyone else for our sins, this book has been about the nobility of being God's people. About example and witness to a world hungering for direction. About strength in the face of weakness, triumph in the face of moral disaster. It is about a God who demands more of us than we have ever demanded of ourselves. About a God who forgives us more than we have ever forgiven ourselves—a God who cries when he sees us fall.

And this book is about hope. Lamentations did not end in shame, disgrace, and scandal. Israel came back from her exile. She rose again from her fall. The nation, once bowed in painful contrition in the dust of the Palestine desert, was restored with the gentle hand of God's love.

> Because of the Lord's great love we are not
>   consumed,
>   for his compassions never fail.
> They are new every morning;
>   great is your faithfulness.
> I say to myself, "The Lord is my portion;
>   therefore I will wait for him."

This too is our song.

And with that hope comes assurance of our own restoration when we turn back to God.

> I called on your name, O Lord,
>   from the depths of the pit.
> You heard my plea: "Do not close your ears
>   to my cry for relief."
> You came near when I called you,
>   and you said, "Do not fear."

This too is our prayer.

Perhaps nothing could be a more uplifting and fitting conclusion for our time of spiritual renewal together than Jude's doxology: "To him who is able to keep you from falling and to present you before his glorious presence without fault and with great joy—to the only God our Savior be glory, majesty, power and authority, through Jesus Christ our Lord, before all ages, now and forevermore! Amen."

And God's spiritual leaders, together with all who follow in their noble, if struggling, footsteps, said, "Amen."

Looking Within

• Re-read the excerpts from Lamentations, reading as if you yourself were the deserted city and the one for whom God's compassion never fails. Do you not have renewed appreciation for how God fills your emptiness and heals your brokenness?

• Could you characterize your life as one of daily submission, confession, and repentance?

• Do you take full responsibility for who you are before God, or are you prone to blame others—perhaps parents or a spouse—for who you are and how you live your life?

• Can you think of someone who has fallen into sin because of something you have done or perhaps failed to do? Would this not be a good time to share your concern for them?

• In what ways has this reading been a time of personal renewal for you? What changes do you need to make in your life? What new resolve will call you to a higher walk with God?

Other Good
Harvest House Reading

THE NARRATED BIBLE—In Chronological Order
by *F. LaGard Smith*

Dr. Smith's narrative combines with the New International Version in chronological order to guide you easily through the incredible unfolding drama from Creation to Revelation. Reading sections for each day of the year.

THE INTIMATE JESUS
Come to Know Jesus Like You've Never Known Him Before
by *F. LaGard Smith*

Spend one month getting to know Jesus as you've never known Him before. With these 31 daily devotionals, you'll capture the entire scope of Jesus' ministry in one unified, chronological presentation of the Gospels of Matthew, Mark, Luke, and John. F. LaGard Smith, compiler of *The Narrated Bible*, invites you to get into the heart of the Gospels and learn how your life can be enriched and changed through Jesus' life and teaching.

OUT ON A BROKEN LIMB
by *F. LaGard Smith*

Millions of people have been exposed to the teachings of reincarnation, Eastern mysticism, and the New Age Movement through actress Shirley MacLaine's autobiography *Out on a Limb*. F. LaGard Smith explores the biblical meaning of life and afterlife in this answer to the MacLaine book.

THE NAKED CHURCH
by *Wayne Jacobsen*

Clothed in expensive architecture, elaborate programs, and impressive statistics, the modern church has all too often traded the presence of God for the nakedness of religious form. Jacobsen gives a clear and inspiring view of what true intimacy with God entails and offers a blueprint that every person can use to build that intimacy.

GOD'S BEST FOR MY LIFE
by *Lloyd John Ogilvie*

Not since Oswald Chambers' *My Utmost for His Highest* has there been such an inspirational yet easy-to-read devotional. Dr. Ogilvie provides guidelines for maximizing your prayer and meditation time.

A CALL TO DISCERNMENT
Distinguishing Truth from Error in the Contemporary Church by *Jay Adams*

Many Christians are confused by recent scandals involving noted Christian personalities. They are wondering how to evaluate what is from God and what is simply the invention of man. Dr. Jay Adams, noted biblical counselor and author of more than 50 books, has written a much-needed examination of the subject of spiritual discernment. He outlines step by step how anyone can take a teaching by any preacher or Bible teacher and examine the Scriptures to discern whether that statement accurately reflects God's Word.

Dear Reader:

We would appreciate hearing from you regarding this Harvest House nonfiction book. It will enable us to continue to give you the best in Christian publishing.

1. What most influenced you to purchase *Fallen Shepherds, Scattered Sheep*?
   - ☐ Author
   - ☐ Subject matter
   - ☐ Backcover copy
   - ☐ Recommendations
   - ☐ Cover/Title
   - ☐ _____

2. Where did you purchase this book?
   - ☐ Christian bookstore
   - ☐ General bookstore
   - ☐ Department store
   - ☐ Grocery store
   - ☐ Other

3. Your overall rating of this book:
   - ☐ Excellent ☐ Very good ☐ Good ☐ Fair ☐ Poor

4. How likely would you be to purchase other books by this author?
   - ☐ Very likely
   - ☐ Somewhat likely
   - ☐ Not very likely
   - ☐ Not at all

5. What types of books most interest you?
   (check all that apply)
   - ☐ Women's Books
   - ☐ Marriage Books
   - ☐ Current Issues
   - ☐ Self Help/Psychology
   - ☐ Bible Studies
   - ☐ Fiction
   - ☐ Biographies
   - ☐ Children's Books
   - ☐ Youth Books
   - ☐ Other _____

6. Please check the box next to your age group.
   - ☐ Under 18
   - ☐ 18-24
   - ☐ 25-34
   - ☐ 35-44
   - ☐ 45-54
   - ☐ 55 and over

Mail to: Editorial Director
Harvest House Publishers
1075 Arrowsmith
Eugene, OR 97402

Name _____

Address _____

City _____ State _____ Zip _____

Thank you for helping us to help you in future publications!